Leadership Demystified

Leadership Demystified

Dr. S. Prabakar Kamath

I.K. International Pvt. Ltd.
NEW DELHI

Published by
I.K. International Pvt. Ltd.
S-25, Green Park Extension
Uphaar Cinema Market
New Delhi–110 016 (India)
E-mail:info@ikinternational.com
Website: www.ikbooks.com

ISBN: 978-93-84588-42-7

Published by Krishan Makhijani for I.K. International Pvt. Ltd., S-25, Green Park Extension, Uphaar Cinema Market, New Delhi–110 016 and Printed by Rekha Printers Pvt. Ltd., Okhla Industrial Area, Phase II, New Delhi–110 020.

Dedicated to

My beloved ones

Foreword

Having written a Foreword for his earlier book in 2008, I am happy to give this Foreword to Dr. Prabakar Kamath's new book, "Leadership Demystified".

Dr. Kamath has brought to this book his core strengths of focus; simplicity; and practicality. Many readers would have heard calls in recent years - "Don't just be a Manager. Be a Leader". Since Leadership became a visible topic, there have been many books and articles on the theme. As in many subjects, especially social sciences, and within that, Management, there have been both deep meaningful concepts, as well as a lot of jargon on leadership. Books also tend to be long. Often, unnecessarily so. Dr. Kamath's book can help the modern, busy potential reader in many ways. The word "demystified" in the title itself may be encouraging, for many readers who may be confused, disappointed, and even irritated by much verbiage on leadership. Second, it is a slim volume. Could be read fast. On a weekend. On a work trip, etc. The "Contents" page would give further confidence. Dr. Kamath has focused on three important dimensions of leadership - self, relationship, and emotional maturity. So, reading can be focused. Need based. One does not have to read through from the beginning to the end. If the reader feels that she/he is relatively strong in two of the above three aspects, she can read and work on the third, weaker aspect. She need not stop there. She can, then self-evaluate on the other two sections; and catch up on the weaker of the two. One could still read the third part for reinforcement.

Even those who have been very successful in their leadership roles could benefit from reading the book. What one has done well, intuitively, becomes clearer. It is more repeatable, in future situations, with necessary adaptations. Besides, we know that past learning does not always stay fully with us. Some, periodic, re-learning is useful. Also, past knowledge may not be fully valid, in changing circumstances. So, some unlearning is needed. Besides, with continuous changes in the external environment, and in the internal organizational environment, some new learning is called for. Dr. Kamath's book can meet all these needs.

Every section of the book has a common structure, which makes for easy reading and reference. The structure contains an actual example: its analysis, implications, a table of attitudes, skill, and knowledge, and "Top Tips". Some may overtly call such efforts simplistic. But, even many of them, when they actually read such digestible material, will find it useful and relevant.

I wish the readers all success in reading the book and making themselves even more effective in their current and future leadership roles.

New Delhi
Nov. 2015

Dr. M.B. Athreya
Management Advisor

Preface

Some people make complex things simple and some make simple things sound complex. This entire book is based on the fundamental philosophy of making things simple. The faith the author has is also that greatness is always hidden in simple things practiced to the core. Mahatma Gandhi was the person we could draw inspiration from. Many managers in their career journey do not have the good luck of expensive education and the privilege of going to the best of Business schools. Yet they are expected to rub shoulders with a cross section of professionals from divergent backgrounds. On occasions, they feel left out in the jargon driven world and struggle with some conceptual gap about what is spoken in common forums. This book is a compilation of various lessons from a practicing manager's life journey. The underlying principle that has made the author write this book is that, *"life is simple and all great things are hidden in simple things and certainly not in great things"*. Many of us can live great life and be blissful. This book is intended for anyone who wants to understand this principle of simplicity at self level and disseminate the same to one and all. I have attempted to share all that he has learnt in his lifetime in the simplest manner possible. Understanding leadership with an uncomplicated approach is the attempt of this book. I would welcome feedback so that we can try to simplify its meaning and approach. I have also drawn inspiration from Gandhian philosophies of simplicity as key to life. Few others who have inspired me are Lal Bhadur Shashtri and some saints whose lives are embedded in the principle of simplicity.

The book has broadly three dimensions of leadership practices to focus around

1. Personal effectiveness: All that a person needs to work at self level.

2. Interpersonal effectiveness: All that matters when a person is in contact with another person on and off the work world.
3. Leadership effectiveness: When the learner is in a leadership role, some fundamental issues continue to pose challenge for enhancing his ability to inspire people.

Many competencies have been taken up and addressed in detail in each chapter. A competency is nothing but how a person behaves to deliver results in a work context on that particular dimension/aspect of work. A competency has four elements.

Behavior: The observable conduct of a person whilst practicing that competency.

Attitude: The deep routed beliefs of a person that support his/her willingness to act in a particular way consistently.

Skill: The act of executing a task given a situation and need. Could be supplemented by the word which uses all the body parts and sensory organs as physical display of dexterity.

Knowledge: The basic body of information gathered from various forums and studies which have enhanced the awareness of the individual receiving it.

The belief of the author in articulating these points is that what matters is

70% - Attitude

20% - Skill

10% - Knowledge.

Any one reading this book should have the clarity of what matters and what is hidden in each concept of the learning process. Hence, all concepts have been articulated with the four elements of Behavior - Attitude - Skill - Knowledge. As a short form we are called BASK P3 competency Modules.

At many places the attempt is to compare the happening of drawingroom with boardroom practices. I believe that we are not radically different on and off the work world and if we focus we have lots of learning to draw from one and apply at the other situation. One can be a business organization another social organization called family. The concept of active experimentation that I suggest is that of feeling and internalizing things so that once the experiment is done it becomes conviction in every walk of life.

A reader would find it easy to read any topic on a given day or one relevant to the current work challenge. The topics begin with a small anecdote and later the concept of that competency has been explained in boxes. This is followed by short, simple explanation of the concept that matters for a practitioner. Whilst a fresh learner is advised to read the book from start to finish, a practicing manager may read the topic needful at any time. The last "Top Tips" are intended for the learner to transfer learning as regards what to try out such that the learning brings the desired outcome. If this effort is supplemented with interaction with a mentor, it will certainly help in implementation journey.

It is also important to notice that all of us cannot be experts in all competencies. It is important that we choose a few competencies that are relevant for performing a particular job. All jobs do not need all competencies is the truth.

Readers' suggestions on all the above are always welcome. I can be reached on my email id: askdrkamath@gmail.com

S. Prabakar Kamath

Acknowledgements

This book has its origin from each of the author's near and dear and teachers, who have enabled all the learnings and hence they all deserve sincere thanks.

I wish to place my profound thanks to my mother who always remained my inspiration in my entire learning journey.

My special acknowledgements are due to my dear friends who constantly remained my sounding board on this effort of mine.

I would like to thank my son who has always been understanding and supportive of me.

My sincere thanks are due to my dear friends Mrs. Poonam Khurana, Mrs.Vatsala Gupta and Mrs. Suhasini Ramaswamy for their unstinted support in giving finer shape to my effort.

S. Prabakar Kamath

Contents

1

The Beautiful Self

Each individual is like a stone, when the sculptor takes it over for work, often the stone is like any other stone. When it is chipped and chiseled there emerges the shape and size of a beautiful idol that people worship and admire. The basic faith of HRD about human beings is the same, all of us are like a good stone, and it is the work of chipping out the unwanted parts to bring out the beautiful and functional self for all purposes. The chipping out part is done through three levels:

1. By one's own self
2. By people around or by circumstances
3. By a mentor or a coach

This chapter addresses all that is required at the self level-work that a person needs to focus on becoming better self or bettering the self.

Learning Habits

"Womb to tomb we are all students"

I got a pay rise, and now I am at a new poverty level. Alas! People say the same in terms of their learning journey in any area of expertise. Wants are insatiable or never ending. It is important to develop an attitude of being insatiated in terms of learning needs in one's own expertise.

Someone asked the Buddha "who are you?" The great man smiled and paused for a moment. The agitated questioner asked him further, "Are you a saint, god, teacher, preacher?". Buddha paused and said "I am a mirror and a student." When asked to elaborate, he said "every day I observe and learn, whatever I come across, I reflect on them as they are, without adding or deleting anything, like a dispassionate witness to a truth".

Somebody asked a learned person with Doctorate "Is there any qualification that is above this and how does he feel having got this qualification?" The immediate response was that subsequent to attaining this qualification the person became aware of how little he knows in this subject and how much more ground he has to cover. Learning is an endless journey and has only a start, in other words it is an endless journey. The belief about this truth is the beginning of a learner's excellence.

The underlying faith is that all things change, hence we need to be observant, learn the change and learn to change.

Behavioral Manifest "Domain Expertise": All the time shows an appetite/hunger for learning and urge to update expertise. Believes strongly in the value of I am yet to arrive or I am in the process of arriving than I have arrived. Shows constant appetite for updating with zeal and quest, explores all possible channels to learn.		
Attitude	*Skill*	*Knowledge*
I am arriving or I am yet to arrive. I will never have arrived. There is always a possible value added to expertise. Faith that what was best for yesterday may	Active experimentation, shadowing with experts/skilled personnel in the given domain. Asking quality questions with quest to learn further.	Awareness of forums and sources of knowledge. Networking on relationships, where to seek know-how. Awareness of processes as to

not be good enough for today.		how knowledge can be procured. Internet language could be googling habits.

So an individual's learning cycle takes the shape somewhat like this:

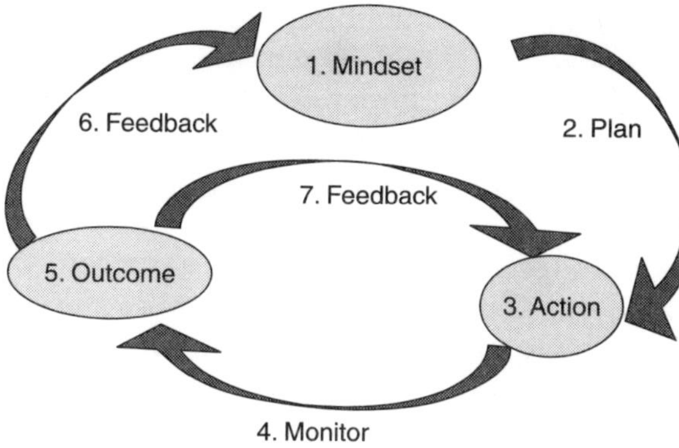

The ability of an individual to learn and how much to learn depends on his mindset. This ability makes him increase his knowledge in the direction he thinks fit and alongside makes him monitor the outcome. If the outcome is positive, the brain is instructed towards conditioning the mindset for further learning.

A student went to a Zen master and said, "Sir I have come to learn Zen from you. My name is Rags and I hold double doctoral degrees one each in chemistry and physics." The Zen master offered tea and asked the new student to hold the cup. When master started pouring the tea it started overflowing from the cup, the student said, "Sir the cup is full – it is overflowing." The master replied, "Yes I am also wondering how to fill the cup further, which already is full with double doctoral qualification. The very attitude 'that I already have big qualifications' is what makes the cup full and leaves no gap to fill it in any further."

All of us possess some expertise by virtue of our formal education or because of our vocation. When such strength is coupled with the inherent qualities of the person it is termed core competence. The truth is that each body of knowledge changes owing to constant research, discoveries and up-gradation taking place due to innovation, environmental changes and resultant obsolescence. There are some Nobel prize winners who are still researching at the age of 100 plus and still feel they have something more to learn. Enhancing domain of know-how could be vertically to deeper aspects or horizontally to wider dimensions. This, of course, is left to the individual concerned.

Anybody who gets into the mentality/paradigm of "I have done it all", "I know it all will do so to his/her own disadvantage." The faith is that a person should be proud and joyful about the expertise that he/she carries. All fields are evolving and constantly updating oneself should become way of life for an expert in that field. Typically, software professionals find that, whatever language they learn, becomes outdated or upgraded version in about 36 months. The learner's knowledge becomes outdated after 36 months. The secret is learning habit to constantly upgrade one's knowledge of the subject.

Evolving and innovating self is a great quality. The essence of success is not access to information rather the speed at which one can upgrade oneself and transfer the same into real life practices. Learning needs an attitude in each one of us. The concept that womb to tomb we are students is a truth. In no domain we can say 'I know it all' or 'I have done it all'. This is fundamental to any person to learn any subject. Given the Internet technology or Google search on any given subject there is so much of information available, learning opportunities have become unlimited. The biggest differentiating factor between successful person and not so successful person is speed at which a person learns. If we are faster in learning what is changing, we are going to be contributors in any given domain. The biggest problem that a learner faces or struggles with is that of the pain of unlearning. Unlearning is nothing but letting go what knowledge we hold to be right.

Top Tip: Skill of Exploring Newer Path

- Can we go to our office by more than one route? Can we take a morning walk by one route and return by another?
- Can you look at yourself in the mirror every morning and ask yourself – "What changes can I make to my personality?"
- Can you introspect and question yourself everyday on one new way to make yourself a better person and one new step to climb the success ladder?
- Could we ask our contemporaries a stock question: "What have they learnt new?"
- Could I carry a new book with me always that I am reading in the area of my interest?
- Can we visit a new website of our interest every week?
- Visit, share, and attend some forum of your knowledge each month or quarter?
- As proof of all the above – every six months if you revisit your own CV how many positive value adding changes are you able to make?

Goal Clarity

"Wind can be of no assistance when the ship does not know which port to sail to"

"If you do not know where you want to go any road will take you there"

The single most connecting point or common guiding theme of all successful people in the world is that all had a goal to achieve. None achieved success by accident.

A father of two sons died leaving a legacy of 100 acres of agricultural land. Each inherited 50 acres and worked hard in cultivating his share of land. They were at the age of 25 and 30 respectively. As the years passed by both worked hard and raised crops good enough for the family's needs. As one person enjoyed the earnings fully with the family, the other spent about 10% of his earnings in buying teak saplings about 10,000. He planted the saplings along the boundary wall of his land. As couple of decades passed by both had grown old and working on the farm was getting difficult and at the same time the family's needs had increased too. As the first chap struggled to make both ends meet, the other son started selling five of his teak wood trees at half price in addition to his earnings and lived life joyfully.

The ability to work on today's routine tasks and invest a little towards future needs is the essence of goal clarity. Doing routine tasks with 80 percent of energy and at the same time investing 20 percent of energy towards goals that is long term and likely to be tomorrow's fruit yielding trees is the crux of a successful goal oriented life. May be one could call it short-term goals and long-term goals in simple terms. A person should be able to differentiate between the routine short-term tasks and long-term goals. For example, eating food and keeping a good energy level is routine task but going for a morning walk is goal for long-term healthy living. Breathing every moment is routine for survival, and practicing (pranayam) breathing exercise is *goal* for life without heart trouble forever. Having found the difference the person should invest time on both.

> *Behavioral Manifest "Goal Clarity":* Believes 'bettering the past' is way of life. Faith that, there exists scope to enhance what was done yesterday and is able to identify and split energies between today's routine and future goals with an 80/20 outlook. Has the sight of goals and proactively does the same well in time without procrastinating or postponing to convenience.

Attitude	*Skill*	*Knowledge*
Bettering the best is a journey. Faith that my best is yet to come. Working on goals is for improving self and, in turn, for rest of the system or overall organization.	Skills to articulate 'what' aspect of a deliverable with 'how' aspects too (content clarity and process-flow). Anticipation of near future changes and impacts due to changes. Alertness, initiative and being proactive	Awareness of SMART goals concept. Difference between routine tasks and goals, strategies and mission in long-term orientation.

Concept of SMART – SMART refers to a set of attributes that should be associated with the goals. These are:

S: Specifically articulated and stretched enough to bring out the best;

M: Means of measure established;

A: Agreed mutually by all stakeholders;

R: Resource defined to realistic needs; and

T: Time lines defined with dates.

This means goals should be such that they can be broken down into simpler objectives, can be measured for comparison with the benchmark; should be such that they are not impossible to be achieved and there should be a time frame attached to the goals.

Routine tasks – smallest part of goals is referred to as routine tasks. These routine tasks further lead to achievement of objectives which further lead to achievement of goals.

Goals: This is a general purpose towards which the effort is directed.

Strategies: These are the general and detailed plans of action directed towards goal.

> Mission: It is a broader concept than goal and can be defined as the ultimate purpose for which a person/ organization exists.

The essential elements of a goal:

- Something that the person is really and passionately attached to from the heart.
- Something in addition to the routine activities that sustain current status forever.
- Something that does not clash with the basic values of the person so working towards it and organization that he/she is attached to.
- Something that is written down and articulated (not superficially remembered or changes in line with convenience).
- Real terms of **what will happen**.
- With flow of **how it will happen**.
- Passion connect, i.e., **why is it important** to the person?
- Something that does not clash with other goals or desires of the person.
- Clearly articulating the end point in as much of measurable terms as possible with milestones definition, with clear dates and appropriate resources allocation for the same. If this is not done it would remain a mental feel good factor or a nice to say thing and, in turn, manipulated or shifted to suit convenience. It is almost like the goalpost getting shifted to the convenience of the player, when the goal is about to be scored.
- Goal should be written in positive sentence as if it has been accomplished without words like "will try to", "want to become", etc. Such that it remains inspirational and motivating.

Dimensions or aspects on which goals could be set for any individual

Be quantifiable deliverable – Measured in terms of units – I will have produced 125% of last year's number of units of output by this date to specified standard.

Be quality enhancement aspect - the manufacturing world calls it ppm (permissible defective parts per million transactions/units produced) - Measured, always by the unit the customer uses as a measuring tool.

Cost reduction for better efficiency - in simple terms - input to output conversion processes - enhance output with same input cost or reduce input cost without proportionately impacting the other elements, i.e., end output

Creating customer delight in a service providing situation - typically the measure for this is the customer satisfaction score measured by a neutral agency or expressed by customer (without any insider influence).

Enhancing service level efficiency - delighting customers or adherence to time lines of delivery eventually reaching the dream of just in time or zero inventory or least time waste.

Enhancing joy/capability development of employees - the rating and perception of people so impacted would remain an undisputed measure of performance in this case. Organizations do measure this through employee satisfaction surveys or 360 degree assessments.

Types of Goals

Personal Goal: What the person wants for himself or herself in personal life journey as an individual. (Example: I will have accomplished proficiency in Spanish language to grade 4 by 31st march 20.. using × amount of money and 250 hours of my personal time)

Professional Goal: What the person wants to accomplish in the field that he/she exists - could be a materialistic deliverable or a capability building aspect. (Example: I would like to have delivered 1 million man-days of training by 31st December 20.)

Family Goal: What the person wants to achieve for the wellness of the family that he/she loves. (Example: Will spend 1 hour quality time with my family every day and build assets by 31st December 20 that will sustain the standard of life of my family members that we are used to factoring inflation and 10% element of contingency expenses).

Social Goal: What the person wants to achieve for the society that he/she belongs to - based on the race, religion, ethnicity community that he/she identifies with (Example: Will create a corpus of X rupees by 31st December 20 to pay educational scholarship to 10 needy students belonging to abc society for years to come. Accomplish this without infringing into any other commitment.)

Noble Goal: Cutting across relationships, what the person wants to accomplish for humanity at large rising above race, ethnicity, religion, etc. (Example: Will leave behind 10,000 long-term utility trees on mother earth for common cause, before I attain the age of 65. I will ensure this by planting and nurturing 1200 trees a year for next 10 years commencing from my age 52).

Top Tips

- Write a goal on a personal front which you think is for your betterment and you really want and think without limiting your thought on resource limitations. Publicize it to whom you trust or print it and pin it in your study table or screen saver. You should keep looking at it as a positive reaffirmation.
- Learn from your mentor or the person whom you consider as role model. Learn from other's experience.
- Write something that you really would like to accomplish in all the above goal dimensions (peısonal-professional-family-social-noble). Place it as screen saver or in your study table pin board keep reading it as often you could. Once you are fully convinced that they are meaningful, share it with your mentor for giving further shape to it. The affirmations and repeated thinking about them would be the beginning to make you move towards achieving it.

Initiative

"Even a mother responds to a child that draws her attention by making a noise"

In a family owned company the owner reached the office early in the morning and wanted to test his employees' attitude. He took a dustbin and kept it at the main entrance of the factory and went to his cabin and sat down to observe the employees' behavior while entering. Quite a few employees entered avoiding the dustbin on the way as a hindrance and reached their area of work. One employee stopped looked around and took away the dustbin and kept it in the corner earmarked for the same. The owner came running and asked the employee why he did what he did. The man said the dustbin was in a wrong place and so he kept it at the right place. The owner gave him a gift and appreciated his attitude. One could call it initiative.

Behavioral Manifest "Initiative": Has and displays inner inertia from deep within in all situations to own up an unfinished task/issue that has potential for further progress given a work context or the periphery of his/her work in specific/life in general. Does not wait to be told and be pushed into doing relevant things. Demonstrates this quality of his own with interest from within.

Attitude	*Skill*	*Knowledge*
Taking ownership in a given situation seeing the alignment with bigger picture/interest. Faith that I can make a difference	Personal organization and ability to recognize priorities. Look/sense around the periphery of the given job/work area.	Awareness that from somebody boiling down to nobody for doing an act is a dangerous practice. Each one of us could make a difference.

Everybody enjoys it when somebody's initiative benefits him/her. But when it comes to one's own turn to take initiative the attitude tends to be different. The concept of initiative is a deep routed attitude, once we recognize the joy of making a difference it becomes natural. Once, a phone rang in big hall housing 50 purchase officers in an organization. Ramu was a new employee and had just joined two days since. As there was nobody around to attend the phone so Ramu picked up and attended the phone. The caller asked, "could I speak to Ramu? Stunned by the surprise of incoming call, Ramu responded, "yes speaking". The caller said, "Your father is in hospital, as his condition is serious, could you please come here." The initiative of Ramu and the attitude that 'Till you attend an incoming phone you do not know how important or trivial it is' made all the difference to him. It is a question of answering the difference between why me? vs why not me?

Getting into unwanted issues is different from taking initiative on issues relevant and around one's own self. For example, getting vegetables for the neighbor's wife is of being a good neighbor (when the neighbor is ill). At the same time doing the same work when the neighbor and his wife are relaxing in their home could become concept of getting misused. A person with initiative has the clarity to differentiate this aspect all the time. When in doubt he/she finds whether the initiative connects to the bigger picture (overall interest) of scheme of things. When in doubt answer the question – Can I make a difference in this context and would I cherish outcome of the same? You would get to know whether you should take the initiative or not.

A learned person was walking along a beach on an evening, the sun was about to set. He found lots of star-fish washed ashore and it was low tide time. He observed a young man with ipod music in his ears, dancing, tossing and throwing one by one starfish into the seawater. The walker asked the young man, "There are so many of them, what is the difference you are going to make." The young man smiled holding one starfish in his hand and replied, "It is making a difference to this fish - any issue?" The learned man got his answer and started joining the young man in this musical dance. The underlying principle of initiative starts from within and with the faith that I can make a difference.

Top Tips

- Look at something that is around the periphery of your existence in the personal life; say housekeeping of the drawing room, etc. Experience the joy of initiative. This could be extended to the garden or housing society that you live in.
- Attempt doing something to a person whom you care and always wanted to do/extend that gesture. For example, reach out at the time of his/her need or pay a visit/call up on phone to enquire how the person is doing, if possible with specific focus to the person's need area.
- Spend some of your extra resources for a needy person. This could be visiting an orphanage or old age home and giving some time as resource and listening to the inmates there.

Time Management and Prioritisation

"Time and tide waits for none. Past is history, future is mystery and present is gift of great truth hence it is called present to one and all"

A young high flyer executive was very busy travelling across the globe on his work and did his best to excel. On his return at the end of the academic year his wife showed the son's (who was a primary school student) home work book. The child as per teacher's instruction had written what he likes the most and what he likes the least.

He likes his birthday celebrations most when his parents pamper him the best. He likes the least is his father's frequent travel out of city on the job.

The father felt very happy that the child valued and loved his presence a lot. A few years passed by - the father had taken a back bench from high paced life to achieve work life balance. One day he was driving down his son to the school, on the way the son now grown up asked the dad as to would he be dropping him at the school all the days during the week. The surprised father replied "yes indeed, this week I am all the days going to be in town and would be dropping you to school". The son was disappointed and said "I wish you had some travel this week too. When you travel mom gives me money for taxi fare to go to school, whatever I save is my pocket money. Your non-travel this week is a huge loss to my pocket".

The father thought he was best utilizing his time by travelling and being busy making money for the family - the child missed his love not the wealth.

Now the father thought that he is giving love and time to the son, the grown up son did not want the time as he had his own priorities. Both ways the father was wrong in terms of his time management or utilization in this case.

Here is another instance of time management. A Human Resource person went before the Labor Officer for an appearance in a case. The issue was that his organization had relieved a laborer from work for absenteeism without paying proper compensation. At the end of the discussion the Labor Officer concluded that the laborer be paid two month's pay as per law and one month's pay as goodwill gesture. The principled officer refused and came back that the additional month's pay was wrong. When he reported the situation to his owner, the owner said that he should have conceded the additional month's pay and signed off. The owner immediately calculated the pay of the Human Resource officer's day's wage + additional day's wage for next appearance + two more day's wage for the work that he could have otherwise done + the travel cost and opportunity cost. The laborer would have also been happy so would have been the Labor Officer. In all, the stubborn officer had lost both ways. Time used or not rightly used is also a focus in this context.

Behavioral Manifest "Time Management": Is all the time respectful of time as a valuable resource and truly believes in "Time is Money" concept, shows respect for other's time and asserts wherever value for her/his time is due. Extremely skilled in personal organization of resources in line with activities that s/he diligently prioritizes. Knows how to say *NO* on occasions that deserves a no without use of the term no (i.e. says NO with touch class).

Attitude	*Skill*	*Knowledge*
Mutual respect for one another's time as an invaluable and	Personal organization and ability to prioritize.	Awareness of time as a valuable resource.

non-replaceable resource.	Skills to say gentle no without use of the word no or negate creatively.	Become aware of priorities in journey of Life and related methodologies of task prioritization.

It is the habit and practice that one has to internalize that forever in life I will only invest my time and not spend it. For this purpose one should try positioning the task in this matrix of importance and urgency. Box 1 and Box 2 of importance only.

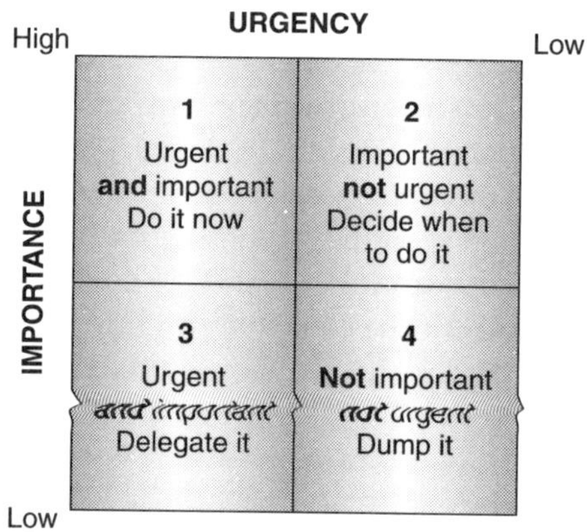

(Adapted from "The 7 Habits of Highly Effective People" by Stephen Covey).

Arvind, a consultant had an appointment with a senior person of a client organization and was to meet that person at a venue at 6 pm on a given day. Arvind reached the venue about five minutes late and did not find the said individual. He called up the person on the cell phone to find where he was, he said he left the venue at 6 pm as he did not find Arvind and presumably the meeting stands cancelled. No body's time resource could be taken for granted. The touch of class with which Arvind got the no without him being clearly told so remained great lesson for Arvind.

Every person in the world appreciates that time is a valuable resource. It depletes with every moment that passes by. It cannot be stored or preserved. Hence time could be spent or invested. Investment in this context simply denotes *that whatever we do, if we cherish the outcome of our deed then it is time invested.* In case we regret that outcome of our conscious act and become aware of such an act that is expenditure of time. Each person in life has only one decision to make, either to invest time or to spend it. Anyone who wants to excel in punctuality and time management has to be conscious of this valuable resource all the time. Great saints call it living the present and every moment of life.

Avijit, a consultant, was called for a meeting by a prospective MNC client for a possible assignment. He reached for his meeting about 10 minutes in advance and informed the reception about his appointment with concerned executive. Despite the prior appointment the concerned executive took about 17 minutes more. As the discussions began, the assignment brief and other issues went of very well and the parties were to agree on the step forward. The visitor was asked would he like to have some coffee etc. Avijit politely replied, "Sir I enjoyed this interface, but please understand my stand that I do not accept any of this courtesy where my time has not been respected." The message was so beautifully delivered, thereafter that relationship flourished with mutual respect with an apology for the mistake.

It is also important to invest time to save time. A young man was gifted a bicycle when it was newly marketed. The young man did not know how to ride a bicycle but could push to nearby places for shopping. After a few months an old man asked him, why he did not learn to ride it? The young man replied I am busy pushing this all the time I don't have time to learn. Many of us are pushing our cycles and keep ourselves busy, because we forget this philosophy that time invested on learning things could save huge time.

Once a lady lost her one-month-old child and was in deep sorrow. Her friends told her that there was a saint who could perform miracles and suggested that he could be of help.

The lady went to Lord Buddha with her child and pleaded, "Please help me in this misery." Gautama the Buddha realized she was pleading for an impossible and would not leave unless he helped her. He had seen the obvious no to her request. He requested the lady, "If I have to do it I have a condition." Lord Bhuddha said, "Please get me a handful of rice as alms from a house that never have had death in his family." The lady searched house after house only to discover that there was none.

A young bachelor had the nuisance of the neighbor lady requesting him to get fruits or vegetables whenever he went out for shopping. One day he bought a dozen of oranges at a high price and gave her. The lady never came back to him with such request.

From both the above citations the learning is that can we recognize our time traps and be clever enough to develop the art of saying *NO* without using the word *NO*.

One can try out the following strategies for this:

1. Start saying "yes": You say "yes" to the request (assuming you want to do it but don't have the time to do it now), and then do one of these things:
   (1) you say "Sure, but I am tied right now – can you get back to me on this in a month or so? I don't want to commit to it unless I can actually do a great job on it." or
   (2) You say, "Sure, but can you do x, y and z first, so we can analyze if this is going to work before we set it into action?"

   In both the cases, you are not turning them down outright, but are putting the ball back in their court.

   (3) "Yes I would love to do it but..." or "this surely is a good project but...."

   But it's not good to defer too many times on a single request, as it makes you look bad. After two deferrals, on the third request, you should give a definite answer.

2. Know your commitments: In order to know when to say no. You should have a running list of all your current projects/assignments, as well as an action task list, made up of concrete action steps you need to complete in the next week or so. Once you see this list of all your commitments, you can decide whether the request can fit into your schedule, and if it's of high enough priority to place on your list of commitments. Guard that list carefully, and only add stuff on there if they are essential.
3. Value your time: Learn to value your time – time is finite and it's perhaps your most valuable asset – and learn to show others that you value it by not taking on requests that don't actually need to be done by you.
4. Be polite, but firm: One mistake a lot of people make is being too nice. They might say no but make it sound like they are wavering. If you respond like that, a strong person will continue to press that request until you say yes, because they think there's a chance you are going to change your mind. You have to make it clear, if you say no, that you're not going to change your mind. But don't be rude about it. A simple, "No, I just can't do it right now" will suffice.
5. Pre-empt: If you think that a request is likely to be made, it's easier to tell people you're busy before the request is actually made. If you're meeting with someone, you could say something like, "Before we get started, I have to let you know that my schedule is booked solid for a month, so I won't be taking on any new projects for at least 30 days." That will warn the person about to make a request, and they cannot blame you if you say no to a request.
6. Never say you're sorry: Again, you have to respect your time. If you apologize, you are sending the message that you are doing something wrong by saying no, that somehow you don't have a strong right to say no. It's very tempting to apologize, I know. We often say things like, "I'm sorry, but ..." or "I wish I could,

I'm so sorry" just because we're uncomfortable giving an outright no. But again, you are sending the wrong message.

Top Tips to Practice

- Make a list of activities that you invested time and felt great about it.
- Make another list of activities that you spent time and regret that you could have avoided - for all these activities develop a refusal statement without using the word no. (For example, an unplanned visitor has come to see you - could greet the person with due respect for the individual and share with him the surprise that you did not expect his/her visit, as you are preoccupied, could you request the person to wait for some time before you could free yourself to catch up with him/her. What you are saying here is, no I cannot be with you without saying so. If the visitor is a great person whose time you long for and that is valuable then reaching out putting other things for a while is time investment - if the affected person is not so saying no without using the word no is the skill. Knowing the difference between these two individuals is wisdom. The skill to be practiced is ability to say no without creating any negativity or use of word tough no, more you practice more perceptive would you tend to be not to force themselves on to you. Hesitation to say no would become a big time trap as others get the signal that this person would certainly oblige or can be taken for granted.
- Calculate the value of your minute in monetary value and display in your workstation/study table for reinforcing the value for yourself.
- Can you make denial statements for the time wasters log that you observed yourself to be indulging in without any use of the word no?

Professionalism

Commit: Deliver
Over commit: Deliver less
Under commit: Deliver more

A person was hired at a million dollar salary per month for a downsizing assignment with a company. At the end of two months he was fired as he had accomplished the task that he was hired for. One of the biggest time consuming activities of a sales person is to collect money for goods sold: this is in addition to disputed collectables. Ask any sales person why this happens, the stock answer is people make commitments but do not pay as committed.

Behavioral Manifest "Professionalism": Strongly believes in demonstrating and doing whatever commitment is made. Shows the proactive ability with conviction to inform authentically what is not appropriate given a context substantiating reasons thereof.		
Attitude	*Skill*	*Knowledge*
I respect and uphold dignity for my own	Sensitivity in doing things aligned to what	Knowing what commitments to make, being

commitments with consistency and sincerity.	was committed. proactively and skillfully close communication loop. • Anticipation	aware of the resources at one's disposal and the process/ skill requirement of delivering the requisite end outcome.

This world has lots of examples of person joining as typists and reaching board room level jobs. (keyboard to board room), many school dropouts becoming the world's most successful and richest business men, a person found unfit to learn mathematics at school level becoming the best of scientist in the world, a person joining as office boy in a company and becoming chairman of the company.

The essence of their conduct is that of being the focused in what they did at every point in time and being consistent in their deeds, call them.

The other key driver in all these persons, which could be noticed, is that of their passion for what they do.

So what is important is:

- Congruence in what you say and do.
- Congruence in what you say and what you demonstrate in your conduct as regards to what your profession professes.
- Congruence in what you profess and practice.

Being a professional is not that of just having passed out of Harvard MBA program or Doctoral program. It has nothing to do with paper certificates or qualification or the kind of vocation that a person practices. Certificates just certify the stream that the person has picked formal education or skills in. It is total alignment of what the person commits and delivers in his/her demonstrated conduct. If there is total congruence in the two, that is said to be totally being professional and mismatch would determine the level of gap in the person's professionalism. We all make commitments on many facets of our life. Do we honor them in spirit, conduct and action? How often we honor and how many times we slip up is the indicator of our professionalism.

If a cobbler in the roadside commits that he would repair the shoes and make it ready for use in half an hour for a particular fee and does it so consistently (i.e. all time on time) he is a thorough professional. On occasions we may have to shift the committed delivery time/standards for some valid reasons, then what matters is do we keep the stakeholder in communication loop with transparency and appropriate notice or we tend to take others for granted.

For want of professionalism in many organizations we find a collection department for legitimate dues, many of us make do follow up charts for many works, etc.

A classic example of the Mumbai Dabbawalas achieving six-sigma level performances in afternoon lunch delivery process is one of the excellences in professionalism. This team is manned by relatively less educated persons and they have achieved this feat much before the six-sigma concept was coined and systematized. What is their professionalism, delivering the dabba on time back and forth? The author once asked a great leader who joined the company at junior most level and made to chairman level position what the secret behind his success. The simple reply was that he has never postponed decisions and said "no" when needed rather than "I will try to say what is possible."

A person aspiring to be a true professional needs to focus on:

- Knowledge: Possess knowledge about his field.
- Competency: Not try to make excuses but find solutions.
- Honesty and integrity: Keep his word, his values and be humble in his approach.
- Own up and show accountability: Demonstrates ownership/faith that accountability always stays up only responsibility and authority could be passed down below.

- Work on self: Be calm, controlled and productive even under pressure situations.
- Image: Carry themselves well as per norms of their profession.

Top Tips

- How could we become aware of our gaps in our commitments and why they occur? Keep in mind that customer is the king. Do listen to your customers about how they experience you (structured stock taking initiative – may be once in a quarter).
- Do we use communication channels to update the stakeholders in terms of slip up? Revisit what you did when you slipped up on a commitment last and how did you handle that slip up (failure to deliver as per commitment).
- Can we identify a role model in this conduct and try to learn best practices to be adopted from such person. Interact and find out why do they do what they do and what are the driving principles/practices they adopt.

Courtesy

"A normal person learns from his/her mistakes. A wise person learns from everybody's mistake. A fool repeats mistakes".

A trainer was once driven to a programme venue by a driver, on the return journey the driver remarked - "Sir you are a very courteous and noble person, this is my observation." In a few minutes of further conversation, the trainer discovered that the driver was a school pass-out and was now educating his newly wedded young wife in a Graduation College on his own initiative. As the discussions went on, the author found the driver to be nobler than himself, and profoundly acknowledged it.

<table>
<tr><td colspan="3">Behavioral Manifest "Courtesy": Carries self in such a manner that is pleasant and likeable to one and all. Extremely sensitive to situations and is experienced by all persons around all the time as presentable person, befitting given any context/situation.</td></tr>
<tr><th>Attitude</th><th>Skill</th><th>Knowledge</th></tr>
<tr><td>Will to double the standards of delivery than following any double standards to convenience.
Outlook as to "I am ok," you are ok towards fellow humans.
Faith of mutual respect as the basic orientation to people relationships.</td><td>Learning & internalizing those valuable acts that we observe and learn from around us that are likeable given a context. Facilitative as to 'how' aspects of any particular conduct.
Unlearning habits</td><td>Context specificity of various conducts that are facilitative (dos) or inhibitive (don'ts). Raising above all personal bias to treat all individuals as equals with least or zero bias.</td></tr>
</table>

The complaint that people have is that of, "I was not sent to good school, my background was this or that, etc." These are excuses, counter to this is that life journey is the best school that exposes all of us to enjoy/experience courtesy extended or shown to us by so many people. The courteous person is one who has maximum of collection of courtesies that he has learnt basis his/her experience and adopted or put to use in his/her conduct. All of us have them in abundance in case we have been observant and sensitive in our life journey. Simple question to ponder - when we enter a luxury hotel, someone opens the door and salutes us - How many of us greet that person back?

All of us cherish the experience when people come across in a likeable way. Courtesy is nothing but that how we could replicate these likeable modules to various situations and constantly make amends based on our experience. This by and large is used in the personal context, when adopted in the professional situation it is recognized as being professional. A learner of courtesy should be willing to unlearn old habits, in view of new learning.

When the author went abroad for the first time, in his morning walk, he found every person he crossed greeted him with a smile. Back home contextually given the variance, he started doing to persons whom he has been crossing for some time and the result is that he could win lots of working relationships and cherish.

Courtesy is not taught, it is sum of collection of habits that we draw from our positive experiences. We liked some one's pleasant tone of talking - What did we adopt from such an experience? We liked someone's style of hosting a lunch session - What aspects we adopted? We liked someone's way of writing or addressing a particular subject matter to audience - What did we put to our practice? We admired someone's way of presenting self - What style of that person we adopted? If we experience such good things and still remain poor in our learning and adapting to changed process, we have none other to blame than ourselves. When we revisit our memory lane of collection of past pleasant experiences, we discover we all have it in plenty. Unlearning and adopting the newer ones is the secret.

Tips for Implementation

- List down some courteous behavior that you liked in others and would like to adopt? (For instance: Best party that you attend - best of the hotel you visited and service that delighted you - A cross cultural family or an organization you visited - what all you liked in terms of treatment given to you - what you feel could be added to your practice.

- Have you replicated your best lessons learnt in your conduct with near and dear ones, and sought feedback?
- Make note of your repository of courtesy that you have been following and you would like to add to - read the same once in a month or quarter.

Ethics, Honesty and Integrity

"Can we differentiate our Right to do from Right thing to do and become aware of Right way to do?"

A disciple asked a saint, who was his master, what is the righteous way of living. The saint replied that, you can do anything in your life with only one condition that such an act does not harm others in any manner whatsoever. This is the simplest and toughest response to such a question.

The author once was invited for a discussion in a factory. He parked the car at the visitor's parking space in such a way that the car's front part was facing the wall. He went to obtain the visitor pass from the security. He was instructed to park the car in a ready to drive out style and then come for pass. With due curiosity the author asked, what is the issue in parking this way, replied the security, sir you have to be ready to leave in case of any fire emergency, etc., and also you should not be backing in case the next car person wants leave in an emergency. Park your car in such a way that you help yourself and do not hinder anyone else.

"Knowing all your right to do a thing

Differentiating the right to do from right thing to do

Doing right things in the right way without being monitored or directed

Making this an internalized habit all the time in all the deeds"

Thus, life becomes blissful for self and all persons around such person.

Behavioral Manifest "Ethics, Honesty & Integrity": In all, the conduct is sensitive/conscious about own needs and sensitive to others' needs. Utilizes things and respects/ values people, never behaves the other way around. Practices socially acceptable behavior without being monitored or guided by some norm.		
Attitude	*Skill*	*Knowledge*
Will to consistently differentiate what are within one's right to do & what is the right thing to do given a context. Sensitivity to one's own rights and that of others/larger system.	Gathering information and sensing/analyzing the context to identify the connectivity to the big picture in relation to the larger system value Vs that one identifies with. Questioning and seeking clarification.	Awareness as to all policies and interpretation/ meaning of value systems of the larger audience. Knowing the law of the land/ society and acceptable norms of the social system at large.

The broad meaning of

Ethics = Consistent behavior that are acceptable to society and the context that a person belongs to.

In other words it is a system of moral principles. It deals with values relating to human conduct.

Integrity = Consistent behavior befitting one's internal mind and truthful thinking.

Honesty includes integrity with straightforwardness and integrity can also be consistency in behavior befitting one's own convictions and values.

To quote an example of ethical behavior: a young Assistant Manager working in a factory on a given day faced a dilemma. He had to finalize a purchase order for value Rs. X. By delegation of authority, he was authorized to sign only up to 20% of X value. Any amount above that was the authority of his boss, who was away on tour and not accessible. He also had the need to release a purchase order to the vendor, who said if order was not given by that evening with 30% advance payment he cannot give the agreed price as it was half year ending. Next morning the prices would be up by 15%. The young executive had dilemma to choose from the below given three choices:

1. Sign the order for value X and promise accounts department that he would get it ratified on his boss's arrival.
2. Sign five purchase orders at 20% of X and get the payment cleared.
3. Do not flout any norm, wait for the boss's arrival and allow the process to go forward.

The executive did step one and went through the pains or challenge of influencing the accounts person to release the advance showing all the prior exercises done in line with norms (budget, etc.) and the overall cost impact of the transaction, if not completed that day.

We all have certain rights to do things (organizations call it delegation of authority) but given the context and the social system that we belong to, all our right to do may not be right thing to do all the time. Doing things well within our rights and checking that they are the right things, given a situation, is all the more important to essence of being ethical. The next step is doing such things in a right manner/process without being told or monitored befitting the situation. In simple terms integrity and ethics is all about ability to differentiate between the following:

Need - Greed
Congruence in Motive - Deed/Action
Use -Abuse
Value Addition - Value erosion
Righteous - Right to do
Contribution - Sticking to Rule book

The true court of appeal in any system takes a few years to give a decision on right things and wrong things. But every person carries his or her own supreme court called the heart or self-consciousness which gives on the spot decisions about being righteous in any given context. Do we hear the inner voice and act or we are wrapped up in our own priority and instincts?

The simplest way to understand this word for a person is that of knowing what he consistently does when left alone without any controls. The second way to validate is how the person goes about making deviations from the set norm given a certain authority and not being supervised by someone (during dilemma situations).

The conduct of the person in the above two situations shows his ethics.

This in essence would mean the person's ability to differentiate between "The right to do a thing and the right thing to do doing the same in a right way". When actions taken with this differentiating factor in a manner that is acceptable to one and all, it becomes icing on the cake.

The path of honesty and integrity always demands consistency from within and some hard work/exertion. Many of us often face dilemma in our professional and personal life journey. Do we tweak and twist things and become convenience managers or maintain consistency in the process adherence yet do not lose the overall goal direction.

Typically, in organization for many executives the test comes while claiming their travel bills (more so expenses for which receipts cannot be obtained - taxi fare, auto fare, tips, out of pocket or miscellaneous expenses, etc.) or entitlements. Even for other entitlements like claiming repair expenses for vehicles and such other claims where fake bills are obtained for making a claim, professional ethics get lost somewhere in greed. Professional integrity always comes from within and not from outside teachings.

The good news in developing this competency is that, it is never too late to start. Like how we clean a dirty room with accumulated rubbish at one shot, we can let go all these practices and define our rights and wrongs and standby. The simple way to set these standards is that of making these standards a level above the norms of the society/organization. The philosophy is that of not having double standards, instead doubling our standards than the rest of the world. Whilst presence of this is taken for granted in an executive or any good human being, absence of this could cause disaster in career/life journey both to self and to the organization that such person represents and sets bad examples.

All the world over organizations are facing various problems of sexual harassment, corrupt practices, financial irregularities, environmental pollution or norm violations. All this is happening because of lack of ethical conduct from within. Everybody things it is someone else's job to control the outcome.

Top Tips

- How do you behave (in terms of time, materialistic resource utilization, in terms of conduct in public facilities when you are in absolute privacy, i.e., the doors are locked and you are all by yourself) when you are not being observed or monitored?
- Can you take stock of what is the non-congruence in terms of your rights and your demonstrated conduct?
- How many times you have been told about a don't that you also agree to be a not to do act.
- Will my parents feel proud of what I am doing?
- Will I like my ward to follow this as an example in all his/her conducts?
- Will I feel proud of this in retrospect if this quality of mine is written in my obituary?

Health

"When wealth is lost nothing is lost
When health is lost something is lost
When character is lost everything is lost"

"To keep the body in good health is a duty... otherwise we shall not be able to keep our mind strong and clear."

A young Indian entrepreneur went to USA to canvas for his company's public issue (American depository receipts), in other words invite people to invest in his company. In the press conference a news reporter asked an obese entrepreneur - sir, if the owner of the company's physical health is like this, why should we trust the financial health of such a company and invest? The fat young man was impacted by this question deeply. He came back to India and got into strict fitness regimen and eventually went on to become a regular marathon runner on all open marathons, of course his fitness improved drastically. The same person's father (the founder of the company) fell unwell during a crucial project in progress. The doctor who came to see him inspected and before the doctor could utter a word the entrepreneur said to the doctor make me fit for work and don't advice me bed rest. If bed rest be the doctor's advice he said let us change the doctor to someone else, who will make me fit for work. Let each one of us ask this question to ourselves, will anyone of us like to face a day in old age that he/she needs the physical help of somebody to perform every day routine – the answer is a simple and big no. That is the secret of focusing and building health for tomorrow.

Behavioral Manifest "Health & Wellness": Is aware of health and the time value and opportunity cost it could add to her/his business/life situations and people around. Is conscious and compliant of input to output principle in all his/her living breathing, drinking and eating habits that enhance wellness.		
Attitude	*Skill*	*Knowledge*
Belief that the mental health and physical is the quotient of one's own making. Belief that I am in-charge of my well-being, complemented by my habits that help my immune systems.	Positive breathing habits, drinking habits, positive thinking habits/positive dialoguing with self and healthy eating habits.	Awareness of wellness related information.

The human body is a gift to mankind. It has all the immune systems inside, if we discuss with a physician they would validate, that many deficiencies get cured by body's natural mechanism and the medicines we consume are only 5% to 10% supplements or facilitators. A nature cure person would strictly feel the previous statement as way of life. We need to recognize this as an attitude and sharpen our belief about this precious gift, such that we learn to nurture this divine gift rather than abuse it. This supercomputer called the body also has its limitations when it is pushed beyond the limits, which many of us tend to do.

Physical health is the coefficient of mental health and vice versa. The easiest way to maintain and excel in this art is that of knowing the basic principle of input-output ratio of life.

Am I eating to live? Or living to eat?

Am I burning all that I eat? Or am I eating excess of what I am burning as energy? Am I using my body? Or am I abusing my body?

The second aspect is that of habitually listening to the language that the body constantly talks to oneself and responding to the same with due sensitivity. This is a language sent by the body through various sensations. One could call it being sensitive to one's own-self and body's language. Animals do this perpetually to maintain good health. They fast, eat herbs, do exercises, etc. The world of yoga has derived lots of postures from animals. In the yoga language they are called *asanas*.

Simple data to ponder:

- A tortoise lives 300 years.
- An elephant or human being lives about 100 years.
- A dog lives about 15 years.

All the above eat and drink some materialistic objects available organically, but the major differentiating factor is that of breathing styles which are entirely different. The tortoise's breath is the longest and that of the dog is the shortest burst. In India the saints call it *pranayam* and have been practicing this breathing art since a few thousand years as longevity secret. For healthy living breathing discipline = 70%, drinking (hydrating) discipline = 20% and eating discipline = 10%. It is said in Indian mythology a person who eats once in a day and practices meditation/pranayama is a yogi (saint). A person who eats twice a day is a *bhogi* (normal liver) and a person who eats thrice is a *rogi* (sick person).

Simple practical truths: All that tastes good may not contribute for wellness. All that looks beautiful to your eyes may not be all that good for your health.

"All that glitters is not *Gold*"

Tastes good + Looks good	Not so tasty but healthy
White sugar	Jaggery
Refined salt	Black salt
Refined flour	Raw long fibre flour
Any deep fried stuff	Any raw vegetable
Processed sweets	Neem leaf
Talking excessively	Listening and talking less

This list could go longer - It is the understanding and practicing/getting or habituating our taste buds to accept the truth in practice.

Top Tips

- Mind your breathing habits - practice longer breaths
- Mind your water drinking habits - drinking at least 8-10 glasses of water in a day
- Mind your eating habits - complete eating = leaving $1/4^{th}$ of the stomach vacant all the time.
- Every day once one should feel the stomach is fully empty and hungry.
- Every day one should sweat once for about 15 minutes.
- Use lifts; cars etc. appropriately do not excessively use them.
- Mind your tongue training. Talk less and listen more.
- Mind your morning habits (take a break and think what happens all over the world in the morning from 4.00 hours to 7.00 hours - and what activities take place either in drawingroom or boardroom and during 1900 hours and 2300 hours) You decide the time you want to be active - This is the major secret to good healthy habits and healthy companionship. Do not argue with exceptions to the rule, look at major active forces and activities that you will be a party to - take your call to twist the daily routine clock reverse couple of hours.

Empowerment

"You are empowered as much you believe yourself to be".

The chief of a police force with intent to control violent mob, gave instructions to use the baton, i.e., lathicharge. As he was the only person authorized to give such instructions, the police team charged towards the mob; some policemen used their batons to hit the misbehaving persons only below the knee level at the same time another set of policemen hit them wherever they could and some other policemen hit at random at the head or vital parts of the misbehaving mob. The question in this context is that, the command given was baton charge and who empowered this three sets of policemen to adopt these three styles of baton charge? The answer is empowerment based on personal authority.

An officer had to finalize the agency license for a company for which the authority rested with his boss. The very next day season for marketing the product had to begin and hence the urgency. The officer made a decision to issue the license himself and get it ratified on his boss's arrival. He thus empowered himself to act in his own way while being within limits.

Behavioral Manifest "Empowerment": Acts all the time to situations as the inner call or self says with authenticity. Takes guidelines from authority figures but applies self level thoughts to context and acts as given situation warrants.

Attitude	*Skill*	*Knowledge*
The faith given a context, I must own up my responsibility and use the authority. appropriately. Ability to respond to any situation.	Judging the magnitude of reality confronting and be able to act with authenticity.	Knowing that situational behavior of own self is important than towing all the time formal lines or remaining confined to the rule book.

Here we can talk about the dynamic triangle which includes challenger, creator and coach. A challenger is a person or situation that forces one to clarify the goal. Challengers encourage one to get clearer about what it is we do want, then focus efforts towards moving closer to that goal. Creator gets closer to and clearer about the goals or outcomes by setting up objectives. A coach asks questions that are intended to help the individual to make informed choices. A coach sees the individual as capable of making choices and of solving their own problems.

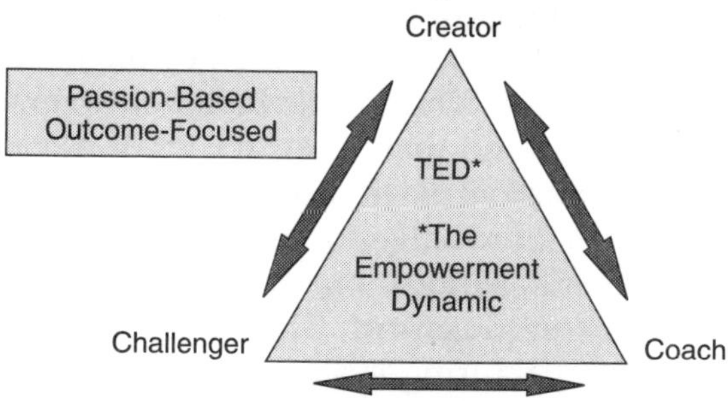

As in the above case the situation to issue the agency license urgently is a challenger. Whether to issue the license, or how urgent it is, or whether it is worth bypassing the authority, all these questions that a person asks his conscience makes it a coach. And one who decides on how to go about issuing it, and exact the steps to be taken acts as a creator.

All of us are empowered as much we think ourselves to be. Whilst the formal delegation of authority is prevalent in many organizations through systems, individual empowerment is more intrinsic to a person at the execution point.

The popular complaint is that many of us are not empowered to do many things and senior role holders (management) control all the power and authority. In the process we suffer due to "poor me syndrome" which in Hindi language is called the *"mai bechara bahana"* and this becomes a persecutor in terms of *karpman* drama triangle. We often nurture these thoughts and wait for someone else to give us the power. By this conduct we make that person more and more powerful make ourselves, less powerful and the person becoming less powerful becomes a victim in terms of *kerpman* drama triangle whereas the person assuming more power becomes a rescuer. When someone operates in such a state, any amount of documented delegation of authority or orders would be insufficient.

Each one of us has a context. Are we behaving to the best of our faith and moving ahead or blaming it on the management is the essence of empowerment. There are organizations where each level of person talks about management until the CEO. Who is that management nobody knows. This is one thought that could tie a person or liberate. The simple Japanese concept of each person working on a job knows it the best. The entire Japanese manufacturing practices revolve around that. The concept of *gamba* - go see things at the happening place, Kaizen - use the doer at the workplace and his knowledge for improvements and *Kanban* -leverage the doer's outlook on the spot with all displays and messages for enforcement. This is the best strength of the Japanese manufacturing system that the world admires. The genesis is that the working person on the spot knows and does the best; the rest could be support systems only.

When Mahatma Gandhi was thrown out of the first class compartment in South Africa from the train because of being a non-white, he also felt angry, powerless and insulted. What did he do with his anger? Did he feel sad and left out? Did he sulk and cry, as to the situation of being powerless? His anger in that context gave India the freedom. With least of experience in Indian soil, he became the most powerful person in the country and could launch a revolt against the British. There are other persons who have shown their power like Anna Hazare who led the country to battle against corruption, the first lady Indian Police Service officer (Ms. Kiran Bedi), Inspector General (Jail) who went on to win the Magsaysay award for jail reforms. This was despite the fact that the formal empowering authority put her in the side lines away from main stream. So did a Chief Election Commissioner of India (Mr. T N Seshan), went on to implement election reforms, which were never thought about before his tenure or thought to be impossible to implement. This he could do despite the govt. wanting to clip his wings with the appointment of two election commissioners as a committee.

Top Tips

- Recall what you did the last occasion when you were stranded alone with no one to authorize an act? How did you act? How differently could you have handled the same = your empowerment belief.
- Attempt exercising your personal authority in an area that is legitimate for you.
- First identify such processes, enjoy your action on them, and then take it forward to high risk areas.

Self Belief

"Each time you fall down, recall and relive
What you did when you fell down on the last occasion"

Belief equals possibilities.

Long ago, a battle was about to take place. One of the generals was talking about tactics with his team of officers. An officer interrupted him and said that he thought the strategy was a waste of time. "The gods have already decided who will win." he proclaimed. "Are you suggesting that fate has decided the result in advance?" the general asked. "Yes, I am." the officer responded. The general took a coin out of his pocket and said, "So if I toss this coin and it comes up heads, we win, but if it's tails we lose. Is that how fate works?""Pretty much." said the officer. The general tossed the coin and it came up heads."See, the gods have decided. We can't lose now!" They went to their troops with the good news and the soldiers marched into battle with renewed enthusiasm. After a glorious victory, the officers met in the general's tent to celebrate."Do you believe in fate now?" the general was asked. The leader smiled, reached into his pocket and pulled out the coin to show to the others. It was heads on both sides. "No, I don't believe in fate, just the value of self belief. When the soldiers thought that we couldn't lose, I knew that we couldn't lose." The general cultivated self belief in soldiers and thus the possibility to win.

A father and a son were walking with a mule having launched on a long journey. When they crossed the first village on their way someone remarked what strange behavior, why can't they both ride on the mule rather than walk. Both decided to sit on the mule's back. When they crossed the second village someone remarked "Two persons on a mule back, how strange, why can't the old father sit and the young man walk". Immediately the young son got down and allowed the father to continue. While they crossed the third village someone remarked "The young man is walking the grown up person is enjoying the mule's ride, how strange?" The father got down and made the son sit on the mule's back. While they came to the fourth village, a person who has been following them all this while remarked, "Poor mule, with all this ride's how tired by now it would be". Both decided to carry the mule on their shoulder. The moral of the story is that on any given subject the rest of the world would certainly have some opinion to remark, what matter is what our self belief on the given subject is. Listening to other's opinion and ideas for learning or balancing our unknown side is fine. Are we being driven by our beliefs or do we all the time fritter our thoughts and be driven/ influenced blindly by the remarks of others around us.

Behavioral Manifest "Self Belief": The individual is clear and aware of one's own worth and innate qualities that makes him/her stand out from the herd. Is strongly driven by the faith that each person is unique and "so am I". Listens and values others' opinion with due respect yet takes what is appropriate in given context using his/her own wisdom conviction.		
Attitude	*Skill*	*Knowledge*
That I am unique. I believe in self worth. I value myself for the good qualities I possess. I can make a difference.	Experiencing and developing positive faith. Sensing what drains energy and skill to modulate.	Ability to gather and being aware of the repository of one's own strength and area for improvement and being positive about the scope in life journey ahead. Knowing processes of gaining self insight.

We look at ourselves each day in the mirror to see how we look like. This may often be about our physical appearance. The other part of our inner self is: "what makes our belief and it needs some quite time to look internally.

Why we find so many mirrors that we see in a gym?

Why we all need time for reflections each day?

Why are that individual goal statements or organizational vision/mission statements are written down and displayed in a conspicuous manner for the related individuals to view them often?

The answer is to reinforce our collective organizational beliefs and not go astray. The highest court of justice is one's inner voice. It is a habit called positive reinforcement and it starts with self, if others around do, it is God given additional bonus.

It is popularly said the *personality* of a person is what others think about him and *character* is that of what the person thinks about his own self. The business of self belief is all about building one's own character that is crucial for the life's journey.

It is imperative that every person has the awareness about one's own positives and areas for improvement. It is a great strength that would put a person in good stead, at all testing situations as it is natural to encounter challenges in life journey. In testing times all persons feel lonely and insufficient, more so when self beliefs are missing.

Self belief is all about the faith that I could do it from a humble beginning that I can do it all the time. When the same thought migrates to I only can do it that could be migration to overconfidence or arrogance.

The life of each individual is filled with positives and scope to improve situations. A deeper insight into this could make a person realize that all of us have it 50/50. The choice that each person could make is that of, to frown and struggle, alternately smile and flourish. The underlying philosophy germinates from self belief of 'this cup is also half full'.

Top Tip

- When the going gets bad, can each person recall what he/she did when it similar situation occurred last?
- Take some time before going to bed to reflect the transactions of the day and match them with self beliefs.
- Can I reflect every day on what went wrong today What is the lesson I draw that I am willing to put to practice.
- Relate to your deeds and professed values - Do they match your aspired image or your apprehended image?

Become aware of where you tend to slip up and talk to your mentor how could handle such slip ups.

Personal Organization

"In a pitch dark home some people can go through all the morning routines and come out dressed up in a ready to go manner others search for their socks or handkerchief every day in broad daylight in their own wardrobe" - Which is better?

A teacher in a classroom demonstrated an exercise as follows. He filled a glass container with some stones and asked the students, "is the container full." Students replied "YES". He then put some smaller pebbles into that container which went in between the stones and filled fully. He asked the students, "is the container full?". "YES", was the reply. He filled some sand, which went and settled in between the pebbles and filled the container – "Is the container full," asked the teacher. "YES" was the reply. The teacher said this still has scope for me to fill some water. The message is had he started with water, then sand and so on, he may not have been able to fill the container. Personal organization is all about knowing priorities and sequence of them in life journey. For example family then, friends followed by job relationship and later the periphery of the place where one stays. Are our deeds organized to this awareness and sequence of resource investment in that flow?

An organized person is one who knows all his/her valued resources and is all the time able to retrieve and put them to functional use that they are intended for with ease and comfort. A disorganized person searches for everything and misses out opportunity and puts others also to discomfort. A personally organized person is efficient and effective in delivering results that enables him to perfectly achieve goals within the prescribed time with minimal resources.

As it is said, "Organization doesn't really accomplish anything. Plans don't accomplish anything, either. Theories of management don't matter much. Endeavors succeed or fail because of the people involved. Only by attracting the right people will you accomplish great deeds." So unless an individual is personally organized even organizations cannot prosper.

Behavioral Manifest "Personal Organization": The person is all the time aware of the environment around and is able to carry oneself behaviorally in a resourceful manner befitting the situation that he/she has been put into. Leverages all the resources optimally in a process centric manner.

Attitude	*Skill*	*Knowledge*
Faith that my disorganization could become the premium of the others. 'Everything at the place and a place for everything' attitude.	Resource organization and prioritization. 5S orientation in all the deeds towards all kinds of resources. Resource efficiency in all forms of usage anticipating time and place of what is required and when. (5S = Japanese way of housekeeping).	Resource being at right place at right time is important, being organized helps the functionality of one and all.

Each individual manages certain resources in personal and professional life. The Three Ms & One I, namely Man hours (time - of self or others around in relationship as a resource), Money, Material (materialistic possessions) and Information base (yester years it used to be papers and documents in the tray and these days it is our inbox and digital data dominantly). A well organized person is one who knows all that he/she has, as to where they are (utilized/ placed or stored, etc.) and why they are the way they are (the logic behind the way they are kept as to easy memorization/ remembrance/retrieval) and is any time able to retrieve and put to use at once the requirement is felt. This needs some logical thinking and respect for the resources and for the efforts that go behind creating them. The person also needs to have some personal style/supported by logical/foolproof thinking in mentally and physically sequencing them. The aspect of personal organization calls for simple to use and remember, understandable to all relevant individuals. The best acid test would be how they come handy during the absence of the person for relevant others. For example, some persons could relate/refer to a mail or information sent to them ages before in no time. The trick is their referral and retrieval system. Some persons could pack and unpack any of their belongings with ease and comfort. Some persons on all the occasions find time to do any activity that creeps up before them.

Procrastination (logical way of postponing a task and justifying oneself to comfort that practice) - Lack of personal organization often results in:

Cancellation of meetings or going late for meetings/ gatherings with prior commitments.

Often reporting late for an occasion with excuses like traffic snarls, I am running late because my previous meeting got delayed, I did not find such and such data, etc.

Missing a train or flight, etc., during a planned travel.

Boardroom to drawingroom these concepts are not different. The expansion/magnification of the drawing-room behavior reaches to the organizational context too.

Wardrobe and workstations are not different in organization of resources. The personally organized person becomes an asset and a person who is not becomes a drain on the energy of others around.

Top Tip

- Could you develop logic for the way you keep your materialistic articles in terms of their frequency of retrieval need, the logic that you find it easy to relate to?
- Could you decide on your life priority and invest your time on first things first basis. For example, family, job, social work. Revisit this also at different phases of life. The sequence could change at 25 year of age and 60 years of age.
- Could you decide that your time will always be an investment into the activities of your conscious choice rather than as is where is.
- Could we observe and learn from a person (whom we value in his/her information management) the logic by which the person stores information. The yester year's executive secretary's filing organization is one way to learn from or a typical unmanned material stores' person's methodology of storing material. Typically, these stores are user friendly for anyone to come and pick material. Now let us convert how the logic could be put to use to our information and materialistic resources.

Could you observe a person whom you value in terms of personal organization as to his/her process/style of having his inbox mail and folder.

5S for Reference

Japanese terminology	*Indian terminology/ meaning*
SEIRI	SORT: demarcating and separating necessary items from the unnecessary ones.

SEITON	SYSTEMISE: put every necessary item in good order.
SEISO	SWEEP: clean the workplace thoroughly.
SEIKETSU	SANITISE: maintaining high standard of cleanliness so that there is no dirt and dust.
SHITSUKE	SELF-DISCIPLINE: following all the above 4S diligently.

2

Interpersonal Relationship

A country wants independence.

A state wants self-rule.

A person wants to be independent from parental controls.

An employee wants to operate independently from the boss's controls.

We all enjoy independence, be it at self level or at country level. This is often because there is an urge to grow and become self-reliant. But the truth is that in personal life we are totally dependent on parents during childhood and in the formative stage of our corporate journey we are on the boss. The moment we feel that we are out of that stage of parental control and have become independent. Soon we realize that we have become interdependent on our other relationships and we have made social associations.

Social association or people dependence starts to grow as soon we become parents in personal life and supervisors in organizational life. All of us want to shower love and affection on our children and be the best of the parent. But the fact is that many parents establish many images in the minds of their children while children are growing, these images being contrary to a loving and caring image. The children gather such images of the parent, because of the true behavior that they observe, despite the loving and caring intentions.

In organizations it is popularly said people leave managers, not organizations. We need to accept this truth that man is a social animal and interdependence of human beings is an integral truth. In the organization each supervisor wants to achieve the best for the organization and do good to one and all. But how one expresses oneself is where the magic begins. Each one believes democracy stops at my level. Here also the truth is that, front end supervisor to board level director all are interdependent.

How does this magic happen?

Who is responsible for this?

The answer is, it is our interpersonal behavior. Whilst the intent was noble and good, the conduct is often not in line with our aspirations, may be hence we land up achieving an actual image which is our apprehended image rather than our aspired image.

The answers could often be:

- Parenting was not taught to us and we achieved it by trial and error.
- We were all the time wanting do our best given our situation.
- Our children were exposed to so many other things.
- We have certain organizational limitations.

If we take a moment to reflect this is the essence of interpersonal relationship building, recognizing the truth that we are interdependent. The myth we had was that the child or the direct report in the organization are totally dependent on us. We stopped reflecting on our interpersonal behavior process mistakes and indulged in rationalizing our behavior to be always the best.

All of us have to have an appreciation for the truth of our interdependence in all facets of our life. The simple truth in each form of our existence we are interdependent on many things.

Role Clarity

A tyrant of a sadist king had the habit of teasing and troubling his citizens. In one of his, such processes, he announced to the country that he would call anybody and ask certain questions at his will, they must present themselves without fail. In addition he also had mentioned that any person, who answers all his questions correctly will be married to his daughter, otherwise will be beheaded. He went about doing this for some time and so many persons had been beheaded to this whimsical process. One day it was the turn of the Priest of the Church. The previous evening a young shepherd went to the priest and told, sir please permit me to go on your behalf as you are wanted and very precious to society. The priest refused and resisted, somehow the young shepherd convinced the priest and got his permission. The next day shepherd put on the coat of the priest went to the court of the king and presented himself for the process. The king welcomed the priest and asked him the first question - Who am I and what is my worth? - The priest replied, "You are a sovereign and hence worth a sovereign" (head of a sovereign republic/kingdom and other meaning is value of ten gram gold coin). The king accepted it. The second question, what I am thinking now - The boy said "you are thinking that I am the priest (as you asked the first question) but I am a shepherd". He threw the coat and stood with a smile. Stunned audience clapped with joy and the king eventually had to marry his daughter to that young boy.

The truth is that we all wear various caps or hold different roles in our life. Roles are all about living up to related expectations rather than in just one's own way or an approach 'one measure to fit all needs' manner. The king could not notice the role of the priest and that of the shepherd bundled in the same person. Many of us move from one role to another the same day. A person is a boss, he is a parent a few hours later he could become a member in a social club and many more.

> *Behavioral Manifest "Role Clarity":* Understands very well what is expected out of the given job and responsibilities. Senses, listens, seeks what people, who matter around (significant others) the job, expect, given the responsibilities and context. Consistently modifies/aligns actions to measure up to the expectations.

Attitude	*Skill*	*Knowledge*
Will to see the contextual need and then accordingly showing willingness to make alignments with expected role. Valuing the expectations of others who matter.	Seeking, listening to expectation (to both expressed and implied) and converting them to actionable points in conduct relevant to context. Observation skills.	To differentiate between the expectations that are dynamic and job description that is static. Appreciation for the truth that the role effectiveness in given situations evolves.

Four components of role clarity

Boss's understanding (role description)	Own understanding (incumbent's sense of the role)
Others' understanding (expectations of the role)	Reality (how the role is enacted)

What you think that you are and what others expect you to be is always a challenge. A balanced conduct showing one's behavior between the two is the secret to performing any role effectively and this is the reality. This is quite different from the understanding of the person who has designed the role (job design/description). The very word role emerged from the practice of drama script, which normally used to be written on a sheet, rolled up and given to the concerned role player. A good role player completely reads the script before performing the role and never gets fixed about his own preconceived thoughts about the role. Because the particular drama scene could demand some finer changes, he needs to live up to the same.

Knowing what significant others expect from us in a given role (other's understanding) is the essence of reading script. Whilst the script is written befitting a story, in a life story the role is always emerging and evolving. Those who decide these expectations are around us. Our ability to relate and listen to our role senders is the first step of role effectiveness. Here we need to be sensitive and observant of situations around us.

A movie actor is said to be a great actor not by the director it is the audience who vote for him as the best and overwhelmingly crowd the hall to see and admire the role that he has played in the movie. Role is not what you think what you should be doing, it is actually how you perform in alignment with expectations of what your significant others (they are the persons around you – the supervisor, the direct report, the peers, etc.) expect from you given performance expectations or business/life reality. In essence, the role excellence is a balancing act between what one thinks to be done, what relevant others expect from that person performing the role. It is also important to notice that roles are dynamic and evolve around the person as things emerge in this ever changing world. The icing on the cake would be how the person does things befitting the context and receivers' liking/frequency. In complex language one may call it "Conceptual Clarity & Contextual Alignment".

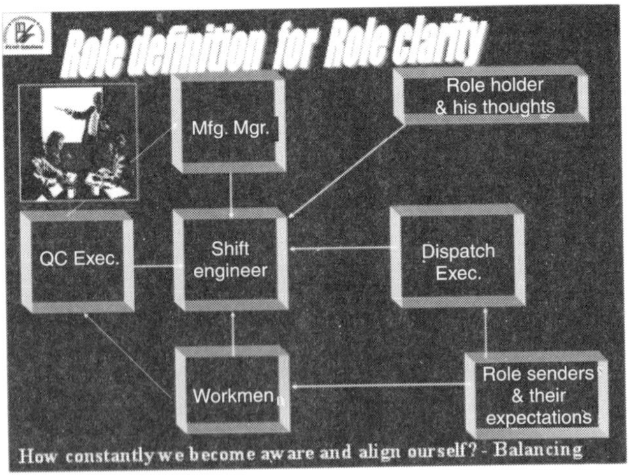

All of us come across supervisors, teachers and so many other role holders in our life journey. Do we value and respect all the teachers equally the same way. Many times the answer is no. Some teachers stand out in our heart as compared to others, though they may all have been called teacher or with same designation. The reason is very simple; some played their role effectively as compared to our expectations. So role is nothing but being effective in making shifts or balancing act from what we think we should be doing in alignment with what related others expect from us whilst playing a role that impacts. Many of us who are driven strictly by the job description and fixed routines, fail to see the beauty of role evolution. The fundamental point about role is that it is dynamic, while job description could be static or may be revised on a periodicity. Roles change every minute or every situation.

Simple example, if there is fire in a building where we are present - our job may not be that of a designated fire brigade person, yet role expectation from us is that we do our bit to the context of firefighting. Strictly we may not be or less trained in fighting fire. The moment fire brigade persons come and take charge; we become subordinate to them without challenging their level, etc. Knowing what is expected before and after the arrival of the fire brigade is the evolving role. There cannot be comprehensive job description on such subjects. Even if one exists, given changing situations they would evolve differently. All the time keeping ourselves aware of the emerging demands of the job we hold at a time is the key. Role players could be broadly classified into three varieties.

1. Person who does what is told as per rule book/job description - fixated and or stubborn persons. The rule book people.
2. Person who plays the role as it emerges in line with expectations or meets expectations - effective role players.
3. Person who plays the role so well and consistently beats expectations. Creates a wow amongst others around who matter to the situation - contributors, i.e., they give much more than what is expected out of them. Those who excel.

All of us admire the third person, because he is a contributor par excellence to any system that the person belongs. Role when played with passion and sensitivity to a given situation, leads the performer to migrate from complying role to excelling.

Simple example: Three occasions, recently the author was called to meet someone at a given time at a given venue. All the time he reached the venue on time and informed the person about the meeting.

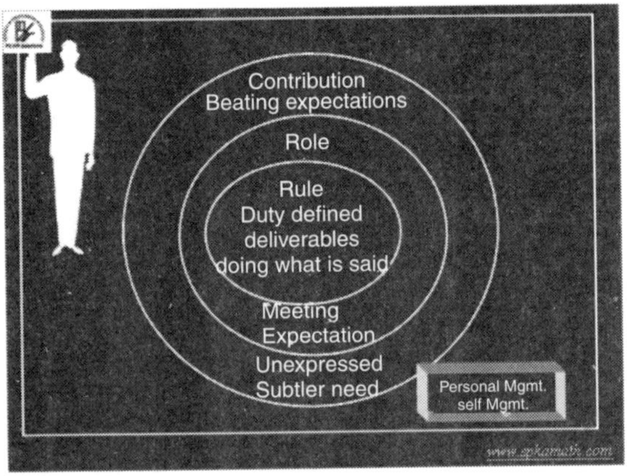

Recently, the author was called on three occasions to meet someone at a given time and venue. The author reached the venue on time. Occasion one – the receptionist said that the relevant person had not yet come in hence he had to wait.

Occasion two – the receptionist said that the relevant person had not come in, is on way due to certain exigency and that the author needed to wait. In the meantime the receptionist would keep the person updated about the author's arrival.

On occasion three – the receptionist said that the relevant person was not in owing to certain reasons, however informed that the author would be kept engaged with some else in the meeting room. The receptionist in the meantime offered water and tea. In the meeting room, the other person had some update and could fill in the author with basic information required as a prerequisite for further progress.

All the three receptionists did their job in line with job description, but the way they went about it given the situation is the essence of their role effectiveness. A good role player is a like a creeper around a tree, it grows and flourishes with more leaves where it has more sunlight and though nobody gives it a predetermined path of growth. The three circles in the above picture depicts that first circle is that of doing what is told we could call this person a rule book person, second circle is that of growing from just what is told to meeting what is expected, we could call this person playing role effectively. The third circle is that of a great contributor who consistently senses the need around and excels in making them happen on his/her own initiative. The contributor does not just meet the expectations he/she also beats the expectation of all others around consistently.

Delhi Metro Rail Corporation began its job in the early 2000. Everybody in the city was apprehensive about a Government organization getting into such a huge project. The expectations from the common man were, it should give me proper road passage, the outcome should be reasonable/ affordable for my use, and the project should end on time. The truth is all the expectations of the Delhi citizens were not just met; they were achieved well beyond expectations. This was the role excellence of one and all concerned with special reference to the chief Mr. Sridharan. In our language we could call him a great contributor.

Top Tips

- Walk around the workplace and see what has changed and what that change is likely to demand in our role that we are currently playing. Do this once in a month or so.
- Talk to people who matter in the system and spend quality time away from the routine transactions to listen to the changes they want in our current conduct or styles of operation/dealings with them that could help.

- Observe how a contributor conducts himself/herself, what changes or styles that person adopts from time to time, whom you experience as a contributor.
- Look at repeating the above three steps at home with your near and dear ones. For example, asking the spouse, parents or children top things that they like in our conduct and top two behaviors that they want to see us change.

Relationships and Perception Management

"Love people and use things
Do not use people and love things"
"Life is not the given – it is
What we make out of the given"

A company was facing labor unrest and the workforce had struck work, making some demands of the management. The company got court orders to the effect that the workers sit only 200 meters away from the gate of the company. Now the Industrial Relations Manager at interest spoke to the local head of the police station to provide protection to the company assets by deploying police force in front of the company gate as provided by the court orders. Despite three phone calls by the Industrial Relations Manager the SHO did not respond. The agitated IR Manager went with the Commercial Manager in person to meet the Police SHO. The moment the SHO saw the Commercial Manager, his tone changed and agreed to send constables in 10 minutes time and did so.

The puzzled IR manager asked the SHO, "Sir what is the secret for your acting so fast". The SHO replied, "Sir we do not know who you are, you also know me only today when you have a need. Contrary to this your commercial manager is a person, who values us as human beings and visits us even when he does not have any work. This relationship orientation of his towards us as human beings is the secret of our prompt response".

Each relationship is a sapling that is grown together by the connected persons and not taken for granted that the sapling will grow by itself and yield fruits. Do we take all relationships for granted and look at them transactionally or we recognize that each human being comes to an organization not just with two hands and two legs to work, but also with a heart and brain that feels, comprehends and experiences?

<table>
<tr><td colspan="3">Behavioral Manifest "Relationship Orientation": Understands the concept of interdependence. Is all the time willing and openly takes initiative to build bridge of relationships with all persons around? Keeps channels of communication open, as way of life. Walks that extra mile on his/her own to build bridge of relationship, is aware of the image that he/she wants to build and is mindful of the conduct with people around, who matter.</td></tr>
<tr><th>Attitude</th><th>Skill</th><th>Knowledge</th></tr>
<tr><td>Open to diversity. Need to belong to one and all above comfort zones. Believes/trusts in inclusiveness.
Will to learn and work on one's own behavioral errors/process slip up.</td><td>Ability to convert acquaintances into valued relationships through extroversion care for others. Skill to relate to cross sections and newcomers without hesitation. Debug one's behavioral errors and work on behavioral amends.</td><td>Appreciation for mutuality and relationship as existential need. Awareness of the concept of interdependence and need to achieve aspired image for self and avoidance of apprehended image.</td></tr>
</table>

One of the great differentiating and defining factor between man and other living beings is that of man being social animal. Thus *major part of life we are interdependent.* For members of organizations it is an imperative fact.

The essence of relationship is all about being sensitive to oneself and at the same time being sensitive to others around. Relationships undergo strain when the sensitivity is skewed unduly towards self only. A perfect balance of both would be an excellent model of relationship.

Certain other factors that determine the validity and strength of relationship would be the mutual respect or value that individuals have in relation to one another. Another factor is the kind of emotional investment that we are willing to make on other relationships that we value. In normal course it is described as mental/emotional bank account of one another that we maintain - do we invest and withdraw or indulge in only withdrawals leading to overdraft or bounced cheque situation all the time.

Some people lose the relationships that are given to them by birth, i.e., parents, siblings, relatives, classmates, professional colleagues, etc., through one reason or the other. Some flourish in nurturing them and also build much more than the given, called friends, colleagues, social/professional bodies and many more. This skill set is popularly called *networking* in the corporate language. But the limitation is that people try to just use them rather than truly nurture them. In life each one has some given relationships and some what they have cultivated.

Many relationships get built over time through perception management. The aspired image of a person, i.e., the image that one wants to create in the minds of people, for example, one's aspired image could be that of a friendly and open human being. Whilst the intent with which the person starts this *perception management* is true and good, enroot people slip up at some stage because their conduct in relations to others. The slip up in conduct often makes the person achieve an *apprehended image* that breaks relationships. This is the reason some time we get feedback as our particular quality to be our strength and weakness as well. Some qualities we excelled and some occasions we slipped up in our conduct in managing our image. Becoming aware what situations we tend to slip up and what are our triggers for such slip up is the first step to bring correction in our behavior. *This is the key to identifying where we commit error in our behavioral processes. The next step is working on our corrective habits.*

A long time acquaintance of the author once called up to ask him if he was free on a given day evening at such and such time. When asked why he was making this enquiry, the person mentioned that he was visiting his city and wanted pick up from the airport. The author did oblige this occasion. It so happened a few days later the author reciprocally visited the city of that acquaintance and mentioned the same to him. The person replied, "Your arrival time is my tennis time, I cannot come over, why can't you take a taxi and come over to visit me four hours later, I may be back home around that time". Obviously this relationship remained an acquaintance of convenience and never flourished. The aspired image of the author was to be friendly person, when perceived that the other person was both locations wanted the author to reach out, the friendly person in him lost his cool and, in turn, lost that relationship forever.

The following diagram explains the same.

Your achieved image

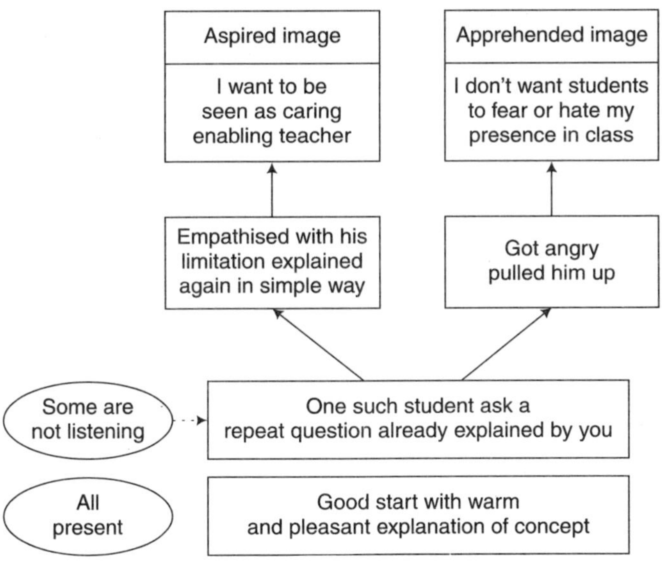

These are occasions we have achieved opposite image despite intent to achieve aspired image. If we recall step by step our conduct at some point we got triggered and digressed toward our apprehended image. This pattern of getting triggered is an opportunity for our change.

Top Tips

- Do we convey our birthday or anniversary greetings or greetings on important occasions to our valued relationships or say, "I do not have the habit of remembering such things."
- Do we call on or make phone call to know how a person is doing. The call is to express authentic interest in knowing health for elders, career journey for mid career persons, learning needs for the younger persons or progress on particular endeavor of their interest that we know off etc. When this is done without any particular favor to seek out of concern-care - compassion. We achieve a special image in such person's mind.
- Can we reach out to the place of a person's work or place of stay instead of always calling over the person to our place of our convenience.
- Leveraging the social forums/networks for various common causes yet not exploiting them for personal needs/greed.

Feedback

"Providing feedback is an art – Receiving feedback is a fine art Feedback is provided only, when solicited".

In the great Indian epic the Mahabharata "The hero, a great archer and warrior Arjun at the end of the battle in Kurukshetra felt that he has conquered and showed signs of arrogance of his achievement. His mentor Lord Krishna wanted to show him that he is indeed an instrument in the celestial dance of happenings. The mentor narrated how the great Karan was killed because his strengths had been taken away prior to the battle in which eventually Arjun killed him.

Krishna gave Arjun the message of Bhagvadgita only after being sought by Arjun due to the state of being hugely confused at the battleground. The truth was that Arjun was with Krishna, for quite some time in his life but Krishna never gave him the message of Bhagvadgita. In other words feedback of life journey and purpose was also not given unsolicited. The precedent condition of the warrior was confusion and he surrendered to the mentor soliciting what to do in this confused state.

In interpersonal situations, soliciting and providing feedback is an integral process of enabling one another. But it has some norms and processes to be followed to be effective, enabling and impactful to the recipient.

Behavioral Manifest "Providing feedback and enabling others": Has the knack to catching people doing right and also skillfully puts area for improvements with observed behavioral data with suggestive options giving the feedback seeker autonomy of choice making. Is never prescriptive, allows the feedback receiver to make choice as to corrective course of action. Understands the sensitivity given a context and acts with due diligence and privacy.		
Attitude	*Skill*	*Knowledge*
Will to enable the other person to see the unseen. Conviction and sincerity to hold a mirror very close to the event, without postponing.	Choice of words, observation skills as to data points of demonstrated behavior without coloring the same.	Clarity of the steps involved in the feedback process and relevance of a context. Appreciation for privacy of other person.

What is a feedback – it is the process of helping the feedback receiver by sharing how behavior as observed by the feedback provider, is productive or less productive. It could go a step further suggesting what mattered and how that could have otherwise been done to bring in better outcome. Feedback need not be confined to only negative aspects of a person (the correct word for negative aspect is also to be termed as area for improvement), normally feedback is both positive aspects of acknowledging a person's good qualities and his area for improvements. Because positive feedback is likely to reinforce the desired behavior, area for improvement is to bring about desired change.

The entire Mahabharata teaches us certain fundamental management principles of administering feedback. Here are the *10 commandments* of feedback:

- Feedback is not given unsolicited.
- Feedback is not equal to blatant recital of all weaknesses or negatives.
- Feedback has both elements: positives and suggestive areas for improvement. The sandwich technique (soft or positive to start with - filling or area for improvement in the middle - end with soft or positive note).
- Feedback should be supplemented by what the giver has observed as to the behavior demonstrated by the feedback seeker in real life situations. Rather than using judgmental words such as "You are bad at communication", "You have bad manners", "You have bad temperament", "You lack patience", etc.
- Feedback provided near (in time and space) the event is very facilitative else people tend to forget or the observed behavior tends to fade off in the memory of both parties.
- Feedback seeker should be prepared.
- "Praise in public and reprimand in private" is a golden rule; hence privacy is essential and facilitative factor in feedback.
- Feedback providing should all start with putting the goal first then the related information that will help goal directed movement.

- Feedback taker has the right to work on what is valuable and keep aside what is not.
- Feedback need never be prescriptive in a 'do it this way' style. At best is suggestive mentioning what worked for feedback provider in some situations for the feedback receiver to explore options for corrective path?

Every manager has to sharpen this skill as this would become one of the important processes to help others grow. People development will not happen by accident, it is a result of sustained effort. In this feedback is an important element. A timely feedback could save a person from repeating mistakes. Feedback could be provided on the following aspects:

- Work performance of a person.
- Desired behavior.
- Positive strengths of the person.
- Specific mannerisms of the person that inhibits others.
- How good things can become great.

Top Tips

- Can we practice seeking feedback from our valued relationship and such that we practice asking them questions covering the above commandments or the sandwich process (reverse process to know how people try it and learn from that). For example: What strengths in me you find it functional to my current role? What dimensions of my behavior I need to change to enhance my performance effectiveness? Could you share some of my counterproductive behavioral instances from your observations?
- Can you observe a skilled person in this art and note down the process that the person is leveraging to deliver feedback.
- Can we observe a good video clip on the subject as there is a lot of quality stuff available in the net for our understanding the basics?

Sensitivity and Empathy

John, a highly principled mature corporate leader, called up his friend David for some financial help. David on the other side acknowledged his willingness to help, having said that David also mentioned that "how many occasions a person like John may have thought before making this request, I feel honored that you chose me". David showed concern, care and compassion in this process and John felt privileged and blessed to have such a friend indeed at such time of need. The level of empathy and sensitivity shown by David was a testimony of their friendship and mutual regard. Indeed John was feeling extremely delicate before making the request.

Behavioral Manifest "Sensitivity & Empathy": Is always in touch with one's own feeling and also recognizes and is respectful of feeling of other's given any situation. Takes the initiative to authentically express feelings with due respect for the person and context that is in front and owns up the origin of such feelings generated in self. Communicates to others with concern - care - compassion.

Attitude	*Skill*	*Knowledge*
All the time is in touch with bodily and emotional senses that arise and pass by composure without extreme mood swing.	Experiencing moment or experiencing an experience. Recognizing the emotions and ability to name what it is.	Awareness of the concept of • sensitivity that brings about empathy; • asset of sensory organs and science behind it. Appreciation that sensitivity and empathy play a key role in interpersonal situations.

Essential words that have something to do with this concept are empathy, sympathy, recognizing feelings and being authentic in expressing feelings given a relevant context.

The biggest gift that one can give to a passerby is to exchange a smile. All it needs is to be sensitive that everybody likes to be greeted or smiled at. Interestingly, this is a quality all of us, by birth, are bestowed with or born with. Unfortunately, in the life journey of being so busy, we somehow forget these simple qualities and put up a face which is truly not representative of our inner self.

Every human being while undergoing an experience does experience some feeling. Ability to recognize the feeling that one has gone through is the concept of being sensitive to self. If we could also recognize what is being experienced or felt by the other person we are in relationship with, that completes the loop of complete sensitivity. It means at all situations we are sensitive to ourselves and also sensitive to others around us.

As children when we see indifferent expression from parents we did sense and recognize. For example, we see them angry we respond by expressing fear. We all were children and did this well with authenticity. While growing up we learnt to restrain ourselves. Let us work on this inherent skill to start with in safe zones and take it forward, to wider aspect of life.

Best definition of empathy as popularly quoted is that of "Putting Yourself in Other's Shoes" – this has to be read with another rider "Before Doing So Remove Your Shoes".

Top Tips

- Touch book – Keep a touch book and note down whenever you are touched by an event at a feeling level and what you felt and did. Read it later how you dealt with it – reflect - is there any other way you could have dealt or seen someone else dealing with similar feeling. A few days of continuous practice could make this a habit in you.

- Ask yourself what happens to you when you see a needy person on the road or a sensitive scene in a movie or TV screen, share the same with someone around you and recognize what these processes are. Also develop an awareness what such situations do to others listen to them.

Delegation

"If you do not push down your expertise,
You cannot expertise other newer skills"

A person, whose boat capsized in the sea, was swimming with the help of a piece of log and managing his survival. He found a boat crossing and the person in the boat offered to help the survivor. The survivor gave one hand seeking help and held on to the log on the other hand. The helping person from the boat tried to pull this person and gave it a best shot, the result the boat turned turtle and both got drowned.

Continuing this story to real life happening depicted in the movie "Titanic" – The lady lone survivor, could *let go* the piece of wood which had kept her alive the whole night and jumped into the sea, took out the whistle from a dead body and blew the whistle to attract the attention of the rescue boat. The rest is history – The essence of delegation is letting go to accommodate more or create space for newer things. This happens to be the key attitude a person needs to achieve this competency. The skill part is that of identifying delegable responsibility and pushing down identified responsibility with appropriate amount of authority.

> *Behavioral Manifest "Delegation":* Is interested in learning newer things by involvement and is uncomfortable with status-quo of things around. Enjoys risk taking and letting things go to people around so as to grab newer things for by doing, experiencing, internalizing and learning.

Attitude	*Skill*	*Knowledge*
Will to let go Will to explore the unknown to add value to one self.	Active experimentation.	Awareness that letting go relieves the person to take on newer things. Letting go gives chance.
Trust in others' potential. Confidence in self to pick up newer things.		to the persons around to grow, creates seamless succession and surplus time to invest.

- What was great for yesterday may not be good enough for today.
- If you are doing something for too long, there is a very high probability you may be doing it wrong because things keep changing with time.

Long ago in a country the presidential palace was so well decorated and protected to ensure the safety and well-being of the president. One occasion when a new and first lady president elect was about to occupy the palace, the person went to inspect the facility. The palace was indeed great to the liking of the president elect, but for one situation, that there was a security guard posted on duty round the clock at the living room of the palace. The lady asked the security chief to find out why was that person there and why he cannot be removed. The security officer's first response was that I do not know this position exists for quite a few years since. When the security went on to verify the records, he could spot that this job was created about 25 years back on an evening. The reason was that day the railing of the staircase in the living room leading to the first floor was painted in black. To caution the celebrities visiting that evening for a party that they should be aware that the paint is fresh and wet a guard was posted on duty. This position continued for 25 years. In the same country the security chief used to sit on the president's seat for an hour, before the president came to occupy the seat. This system is still being followed as they say, though the premise has been cordoned off for security and has become centrally heated, the tradition of the security still continued. The issue here is the will to let go of some redundant things we are holding on to in the name of practice or tradition.

Another simple practical example that each reader could reflect on is that of materialistic possessions. Many of us have certain articles for too long though they may have become redundant. I have a shirt that I have found useful and would like to donate it to a needy person is one outlook. Do I wait for it to become totally useless or let go when it is functional. Assets to activities to expertise we need to let go when they are functional for the purpose not outdated and redundant. The next user also finds it functional when it is given at the right time and not too late.

I will let go things that are redundant and do it proactively before it becomes too late. It is the joy of sharing when they are functional, useful and in turn finding time and space to try out newer things. This approach is true to articles or activities. The fun of living is the process of moving from the Well known to Less known to Unknown.

This kind of movement when forced by circumstances is painful, when done at one's own initiative is very much satisfying and gratifying. This migration is also the truth of the organic growth of an individual. If somebody delays this it will happen as the natural law of gravity. It happens more to people who believe in their capability and that of others as well.

When we let go things, we fear others may not do it as well as we do. Often this fear makes us hold things back. This fear could be unfounded or based on some odd bad experience in the past. The counterpoint to this is to remember that we all had day one, in each subject of our expertise, someone allowed us to have that day. We also committed our mistakes and could grow up the learning curve. To overcome this fear, the delegator has three options.

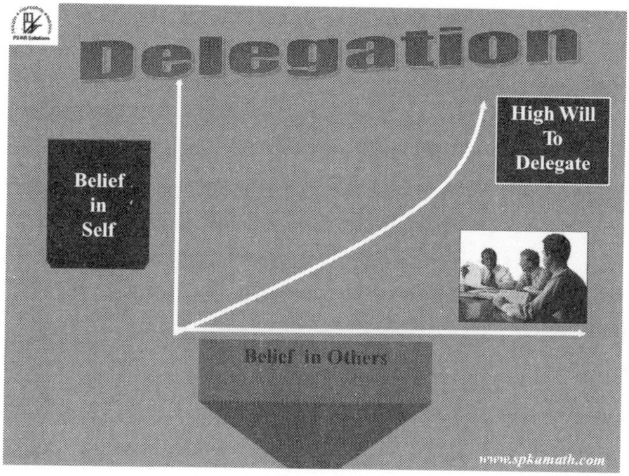

- Delegate and stay hands free: When the belief in the delegatee is high and the delegator's self belief is also high to handle the end outcome. This is like a plane in auto pilot mode. The operating faith is that of "I am around I can handle mistakes just in case they happen by the new person's way of working...".
- Delegate and monitor on a need to know basis: Review of weekly report once in a way checking or asking 'may I help you' kind of outlook. The delegator has belief in both but paces it appropriately to migrate to autopilot level over time. The delegate is up the learning curve, may need help on a need to know basis in a non-threatening way = the operating faith. The delegator has let go things yet monitors in an appropriate manner.
- Delegate and micromanage: The delegator has less belief in self and that of others to whom he has delegated, maybe he is a beginner. The delegate is incompetent and may commit a blunder, if not helped on a constant basis = the operating faith. The delegator's faith that the new person needs lots of help.

The essence of the above three is based on the delegator's understanding about the person whom he/she is delegating to. The wrong model to wrong persons could cause confusion and frustration to one and all. Understanding the delegatee's context is very important to adopt appropriate style befitting the situation.

Top Tip

- Recall what happened when you were completely absent in a situation for some valid reasons. After that what your observations were and what process improvements that you brought about to make the system more process dependent.
- Look at how people cope with calamity situations and draw your learning.
- Make a list of things that you could let go and phase them out at your pace. Take stock how have you gone about letting them go. This could be done both on professional and personal front. Then make a list of items/activities to let go at the beginning of, say each year and implement.

Accountability and Responsibility

"Authority is that, it is all pervasive and all restrictive"

Mr. Raja was one day starting his motorbike to go to office. He found his 12-year-old son playing cricket by the roadside with his friends. As Raja left a few minutes later the ball hit the glass window of the neighbor. The neighbor came looking for Raja. As Raja was out of home, the person found the old retired person (Raja's dad) sitting and reading newspaper in the easy chair. He complained to him the happening and the grand old man apologized to the neighbor and agreed to get the glass changed in the next few hours and did so. In the evening when Raja came the father told the son about his grandson's deed and requested that Raja pays the money to the shopkeeper who fitted the glass.

The ability to respond to the situation of the grand old man given Raja's absence was perfect in the context. He no way could deny his accountability to the neighbor though the child was not his son. It is important to note that accountability always stays up.

The responsibility to pay for the son's cause was indeed with Raja, as and when he returned. Raja had the authority to restrain his son playing by the roadside or allow him to do so and own up for the likely consequences. If he shows the ability to respond to such consequences - Raja is said to be a responsible person.

The above example can be viewed in organizational terms as grandpa being the boss's boss, Raja being the boss and son being the direct report (the word subordinate is deliberately avoided here). The top boss is accountable for his team to someone outside the organization and the boss is responsible for his subordinate's deeds.

Certain basics: Accountability always stays up or flows upward do not get pushed down. Accountability = Ability to account for each and every resource at one's disposal.

Responsibility: Flows down with commensurate authority. Normally, responsibility and authority need to be equal and in case of any imbalance the responsible person takes it on and later seeks/makes amends. Responsibility = Ability to respond to given a situation with equal authority or seek the same consequent to performance.

Success has too many owners but failures become orphans. With many organizations, if asked for the decision or root cause in case of any tough decision or any failure: the common response would be that it is better known to the management. For any success, there would be too many takers who claim to have contributed for the same. Owning up accountability for a failure is a habit many need to work at one's own attitude of looking at such situations. The best example: ask any employee who is the management, up to CEO level people look further up. This simply means nobody. Authority without responsibility is luxury in real life. Where-ever there is mismatch, corruption and inefficiency erupts or creeps. The political scenario in various countries is a classic example in this case.

Behavioral Manifest of "Accountability & Responsibility as competency": Seeks to know what to do and lives up to that all the time. Expresses frankly with ownership and expresses self, authentically given an action taken or in case of failure.		
Attitude	*Skill*	*Knowledge*
Will to own the consequences of each act. Trust that each individual causes certain outcome by his/her action or inaction	Sensing, cost and cause of each action and inaction.	Awareness that every authority comes with responsibility. Understanding that clamor for more authority with less responsibility is against reality.

What we do, in life, has an outcome. A responsible person is one who is able to own up the repercussions of his/her deed. Being selective in this context and owning up good outcome, finding excuses for the negative outcome is the result of lack of responsibility. Here, such a person lacks the ability to respond to the situation created by him/her.

Way to righteous life "Dharam ka marg" – A disciple asked a saint, his master what is the righteous way in life to live. The saint replied that you can do anything in life with only one condition that such an act does not harm anybody. The simplest and toughest definition of such a great topic. Authority is all pervasive as to anything you want to do and restrictive to the extent that you can own up the consequences.

We all have certain rights to do things but given the context and the social system that we belong to all of them may not be right all the time. Doing things well within our right - checking are they the right things, given a situation, it is all the more important to understand the essence of exercising one's authority. Icing on the cake would be doing the same in a right or befitting manner; i.e. way of doing should be acceptable to one and all given the context.

= to see things as they are) meditation sessions widely practiced to-date.

(a) All existential things in this world are impermanent or only truth is that all are impermanent existence.

(b) The spiritually matured mind has to be trained to remain neutral to this truth of impermanence. In other words one need not get excited positively or negatively to worldly happenings as it is natural for all events to arise and pass away. The pendulum of our mind has to remain neutral without the wildest positive or negative swing = balanced mind with equanimity to the truth of impermanence.

A spiritually enriched or evolved person is more at harmony with self with zero agitation with worldly happenings. When the Buddha was asked about what he gained through his meditation and practices, he replied I gained nothing, but I certainly lost my anger, my jealously, my craving, my greed, my mind chatter, my insecurity, depression, fear of old age and death - as a result I can reflect and see things as they are without any addition or deletion.

In the great epic the Mahabharata, the confused hero Arjun was taught just that as the ultimate sermon called the Bhagvadgita - the song of truth sung by the God himself. In essence the God and mentor told the warrior to practice his duty with zero expectations on the outcome. As the outcome of many activities is a result of so many contributors and forces operating in the celestial dance and hence you do not have to worry for the positive or negative outcome - one should do one's bit with total devotion, i.e., Nishkam karma yog - Doing duties with complete dedication with zero expectation.

When we buy a burger in a restaurant, having paid for it, we normally call it ours. Whilst physically and financially it belongs to us, the effort gone into the making of the same is that of so many persons in the universe. The wheat growing farmer, transporter, flour mill person, to the delivery person, etc. So many persons have contributed in the making of the same. I paid for it, hence it is mine is the simple way of looking at it transactionally. It is the connivance of all the forces in the universe that it has reached our hand; this is the evolved way of looking at the same, popular saying in Hindi says, "On every grain it is written where and whom it should reach."

Behavioral Manifest of this Competency: Shows composure in all situations. Is all the time at harmony with happenings around without showing agitation or excitement? Demonstrates neutral or equanimous view to every situation.		
Attitude	*Skill*	*Knowledge*
Belief in the truth of impermanence as the only constant. Will to practice mind training in a steadfast manner to remain neutral. Will to work towards zero or nil mind flutter.	Practices the skill of meditation or mind training as often as possible in any given free time. Ability to reflect and listening to self or the mind chatter during quite time.	Understanding that the issues around the world arise due to one's own subjective views and perceptions. Secret is to work on self rather than projecting on others.

Certain essential elements of the spiritual quotient:-

- A toughest and easiest topic on earth is this.
- It is all pervasive and belongs to all religions and faith.
- It is nothing specific about doing or performing any particular ritual.
- It is not time bound or to be timed for a phase or stage a person's life - can be practiced any time and by any person at any stage.
- It creates harmony with the larger system cutting across living beings.
- An atheist can also excel in this competency.

The work here is centered around self and not on others. If others around get inspired or motivated because of this conduct, it is a byproduct or a rub-off effect. Being spiritual means being sensitive to what is happening inside one's own self and be able to remain detached to those happenings like a dispassionate witness of that truth.

Whilst writing this topic one evening the author was sitting in a session with his mentee. The mentee went out for a few minutes to meet with her seniors. She came back in tears stating that she has resigned due to some discomforting reasons. As this sharing and caring experience was going on the author was feeling concerned for his mentee, etc. Just then the author got a phone call conveying a message that his nearest relative had just passed away. In about ten minutes later the author got another message that he had become a grandfather to a newly born baby boy. All this happened in about twenty-five minutes of interval. The conclusion that one has to make was that all the three happenings are the truth of impermanence; if the mind could be trained to remain neutral every person could attain more poise and balance. With due humility the author realized his being a student in this context.

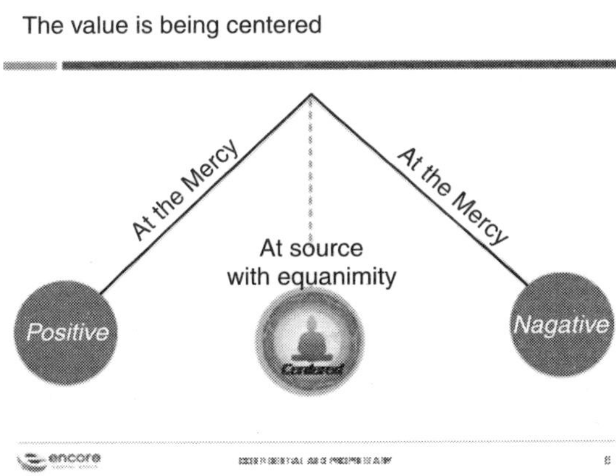

Before going to an operation theater all the entrants including the nurse, doctor, patient are made ready in terms of their hygiene, etc. Similarly, before entering into spiritual journey a person has to make his/her mental hygiene preparedness for the launch. A spiritually evolved person practices the following three processes in his life as an internalized and institutionalized way of life. This is the way one can prepare self level hygiene before launch of the journey. This is put simply by the Vedas as *atma* surrendering to the *paramatma*. It means that *atma,* i.e., the inner soul in self unconditionally surrendering to the *paramatma,* i.e., Omnipresent divine in the celestial force of everything around us. The only thing that a spiritually evolved person can pray and request from the Almighty is also restricted to *"Sarve Jano Sukino Bhavanthu"* - Meaning, let all the living beings be happy. In doing this the following aspects of conduct are important facilitators. The logic is simple the divine is omnipresent; hence the surrendered self which has merged with the divine is also omnipresent which in turn justifies the wish of *sarve jano sukino bhavanthu.*

A person involved in this journey needs to practice the following three.

Nishtha: Doing things with dedication and complete attitude of focused ownership. In other words it is action with dedication and focus to any activity that you commit or living the present in totality with 100% focus. Not in the past or about the future.

Nirbhar: Appreciating and respecting dependence on the processes that are time tested and calibrated and that we have adapted ourselves to or surrendered ourselves to. These processes are learnt and chosen by the practitioner at his/her free will. The archer Arjun of the Mahabharata was the example of complete surrender to the battle processes as taught by his mentor.

Nirbhai: Enjoy blissful existence with zero fear or apprehensions.

For example, Padma Bhushan, Mr. Shridharan of the Delhi Metro Rail Corporation, was very committed and focused on the task of on-time delivery of the Delhi Metro project and he worked hard at a very elderly age. A person catching fish with a fishing rod also has to surrender to the process the same way.

His orientation was to follow the time tested civil engineering project execution processes himself and enable his team to follow. His entire team sublimated to the processes that they defined and agreed to. The outcome was delivery of world class metro rail to the citizens of Delhi on time or often ahead of time with no fear or apprehension of the results.

The end outcome was respect for the DMRC team and Mr. Shridharan went up in the minds of people and he became a role model for project execution in the nation. It is all his Nishta–Nirbharta-Nirbhaita = Blissful living or blissful existence.

Spiritual quotient is all about mind training and mind training in other words is looking inwardly and working on one's self.

Top Tip

- Each person could spend some quite time each day on reflection.
- Reflections should facilitate the mind and outlook to make some alignment shifts from the positions taken.
- The training here is to say to one's own mind that all happenings are impermanent and have the nature of arising and passing by, I will train my mind to remain neutral to these events.
- Each existential process is the moment of truth embedded with the underlying philosophy of impermanence. Keep conversing this to yourself all the time to attain a neutral mind.

3

Emotional Maturity and Intelligence

Recently the airline industry has started announcing on landing that the aircraft has left the active runway and the passengers are free to use their mobile phones. Hitherto, it has been the other way around and has been a frustration for the airlines crew and the passengers. Both the parties struggled in controlling their emotions.

When the author's father passed away his sister who happens to be only daughter and the most loved one did not cry in a sudden shock. After three days every night she would wake up in mid night sleep and scream that he is calling me. It took a few sessions of her crying and giving vent to her sadness for her to become normal.

In both the above situations, the process of choking or channelizing is a choice that was essential for ease and comfort. The truth is also that such things do occur in each person's life. Becoming aware of what various emotions are and what one is experiencing at a point of time = emotional literacy or awareness. The functionality is all about channelization of emotions. Experiencing emotions is natural; channelizing them functionally or otherwise is the process of attaining emotional maturity.

Behavioral Manifest of this Competency: Believes in authentically expressing feeling with due balance of sensitivity to own feeling and that of others around befitting a given situation. Is able to experience, differentiate and recognize variety of feelings, take initiative to express feelings and own up all divergent emotional experiences. Is a willing experimenter and a learner of this science as things warrant rather than being fixated about feelings or being in a denial mode.

Attitude	*Skill*	*Knowledge*
Will to be authentic and interactive in given interpersonal situations. Will to own up consequences of one's expressions and impact of the same. Will to experiment/ explore outcome of the unknown behavioral methods with open mind.	Sensing and recognizing sensations accurately. Differentiating various feelings at experiential level and verbalizing the same with correct choice of words that one and all could understand.	Knowledge about various emotional states of being, the related term that rightly denotes that and recognizing the importance of the same in relationships.

Emotions are energy in motion and it happens to each human being all the time as essence of life is to experience each moment. It is also a fact that every external happening we experience gives rise to some feeling or the other. Science calls it body's chemical secretion to the experiences of various situations as an internal biological mechanism to support physical response system.

Recognizing what is the emotion one is experiencing is the first step forward. This is known as emotional awareness or literacy. This is what we are all bestowed with by birth. If we observe a child back home, without any inhibition, the child all the time expresses the emotions spontaneously all the time. As we all grow in life, somehow we learn to hide or put a lid on this very concept. This often could be because of societal restriction, upbringing, and experience of certain not so good outcome during various significant events and certain patterns of behavior that we have registered as a practice in our subconscious mind.

Our behavior typically undergoes the below given process triangle, of course they happen in a fraction of second and at very high speed. But the movement through the triangle could be all the three steps of logically feeling - thinking - acting.

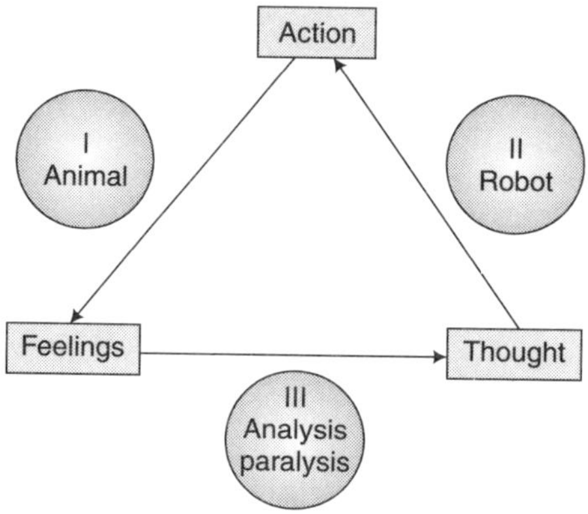

Behavior/Action: Typically any time we conduct ourselves in any particular manner or choose not to act in a manner, we have something happening inside us that could be a logical thinking process. (The right corner of the triangle given above is: Thought). The left corner of the triangle is called the feeling that it generates basis the action we take (Feelings). Typically feeling clusters could broadly be Glad - Sad - Mad - Scared - or some other shades or mix of these feelings. Every action of ours inherently has these three corners or elements happening as a cyclical process. This could happen in a subconscious level at a lightning speed that we may be unaware or less aware. In this process it is important to understand certain styles and patterns of behavior described below in four possible styles.

Situation I: A person at national highway toll gate, wants to go past the barrier without paying the required toll - the toll attendant insists on payment, the person takes a gun and shoots the attendant. The act of the attendant is seeking payment, the other person's action is shooting down the attendant. Let us stay with the shooter's action. What was his feeling? May be anger or rage, etc. The same person in his logical thinking capacity would always agree that it is not correct to shoot a person instead of paying 1 $ toll fee. In his normal element he might even give a lecture how precious is human life, etc. In this case the person acted purely out of feeling anger. Often animals act from instincts and feelings. They are called *reactions to a feeling* not necessarily thought out action = *animal like.* For human beings also the animal inside them at times takes charge and they are not in-charge of that animal which goes berserk. The outcome is always regret. In emotional intelligence language this is called amigdala hijack. That means impulse sensing brains have straight away remain responsible for action without the thinking part of the brain analyzing the situation. Emotionally matured persons are always in control of this animal inside them, they often make it subservient so that it behaves the way they want it.

Situation II: A robot has been programmed to do five acts, when it is actuated, it would do five acts only and nothing more. There are some individuals who also operate like this. *They think and act* like *robot.* They find it difficult to connect to their feelings or over a period of time have conditioned themselves to suppress feelings all the time.

Situation III: A boss holds a meeting and asks for suggestions on a particular issue. There are many who have ideas about the subject, but at the same time experience a fear – will I make a fool of myself? Will I be reprimanded? Will it sound obvious and get discounted – I may feel insulted. Here, these persons experience lots of feelings and have very good thoughts, but this is too much of analysis leading to paralysis, may not make him/her to reach any action. These are people with all rich *thoughts and plenty of feelings* stranded without any action *Analysis leading to paralysis.* This could happen because of some past bad experience and resultant unwillingness to experiment.

Situation IV: If all the time authentically moves through this triangle and will be able to recognize the very experience. They are aware of what it feels like after each action and can put through these feelings into their thought filter - explore various options and take action as the best of the choice that they think is befitting the situation. This is what has been depicted below in the 4E model, later in this topic. Many a times statements are made "don't get emotional" or "it is bad to express emotions in front of others". The message is handle and channelize emotions functionally.

Often when you are asked how you are feeling, we are at a loss to mention a feeling statement, often we respond I think I am feeling ok or I am confused. The very prefix, I think is a denial of a feeling statement, in other words it is a thought statement which apparently appears to be politically correct. The very word I am confused is a denial statement of some feeling that is being experienced but either showing inability to own up or recognize and verbalize it. This, in turn, leads to various anxieties as they some way remain as residual inside one self as un-channelized energy. This is one of the main reasons that many of the jet set executives of the current world feel many physical and psychological issues resulting into poor health. Physical health is often the quotient of mental health.

Four"E" model of EQ

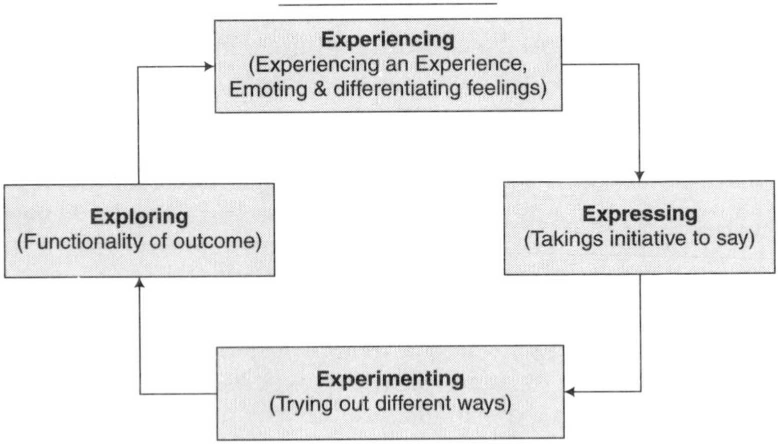

The four steps given about the emotional behavior cycle are about going through the process and each step is crucial and many people in the learning journey may get stuck at one or next. The effort to try various methods and move forward or make new mental models for oneself is called active experimentation. This is the way a child would learn in a laboratory during practical experimentation sessions.

Experiencing: For example, all of us experience various emotions like being sad, mad, glad and scared. Do we have the distinct ability to differentiate and recognize which feeling is being experienced at a point in time? It is but natural that at any point in time we experience some emotion or other. The magnitude of this cluster of feelings could vary. In the jargon world this may be called emotional literacy or emotional awareness. That is this person is emotionally literate enough to experientially recognize what is happening and what is the correct term it is identified with. For example, when we say mad it is a cluster of anger as a feeling. This family could have a choice of words to express the same in differing magnitudes called, slight irritation, irritated, slight anger, angry, annoyed, and terribly annoyed and rage. In a gauge this could be measured as high or low level of anger. Extending this the feeling cluster Glad could have nice-good-very happy-on top of the world.

Cluster Sad could have words like low-bit bad-sad-depressed-down in the dumps.

Mad could range from slight irritation - angry - terribly annoyed-rage.

Scared could words like tentative-apprehensive-slight fear-scared-frightened-terrified.

Expressing: Next step is that how often we take initiative to express or suppress these feelings to persons whom we relate to in that context? Deciding that it is not important to express at a given situation is a conscious call, other than denying that need to express and saying all is well, with an artificial smile on the face is the question to be answered.

Experimentation: If you do the same things all the time, you will get the same outcome. In expressing feelings there is no one method. We have powerful expression tools like the body language, tone of voice, eye contact and lastly the appropriate choice of words used to express the same. Do we think it is only one word and one way or are there numerous ways of expression? We can experiment various methods and see how it works for us. Entire world that we live in is a laboratory of experimentation. What we did as children when we went to chemistry laboratory? We experimented various combinations of chemicals and learnt from their reaction and eventually we made our mental models about the body of knowledge called chemistry. Some of us took it to real life and experimented with people in terms of our changed behavior and reaped the outcome. Emotionally intelligent people keep changing and evolving and become more functional in their relationships.

Exploration: Anything we do in life has an outcome including the act of not doing anything. Do we do things as is where is and leave it or reflect on the aspired outcome – actual achieved outcome – apprehended outcome? All of us work to achieve our aspired outcome. While doing so we may achieve the aspired outcome and feel happy. On occasions the outcome is not in line with the aspired one instead it is something that apprehended as a strict no-no. An emotionally matured person would reflect on the sequence of his/her act and debug- "where did I drop the ball... What is it that I could do differently when I confront similar situation next time". An emotionally intelligent person is a repository of reflections and is able to comprehend what works or what does not. Such a person is ready for newer experimentation when such an opportunity unfolds again. It is popularly said a wise person learns from everybody's mistake, a normal person learns from one's own mistake and a fool repeats mistakes.

Ten Commandments of Emotional Literacy

1. Thou shall not power play, Ask instead for what you want until you get it.
2. Thou shall not allow yourself to be power played, Don't do anything you are not willing to do of your own free will.
3. Thou shall not lie by omission or commission, except where your safety or the safety of others is concerned, avoid lying.
4. Thou shall stand up for how you feel and what you want, If you don't, it is not likely that anyone else will.
5. Thou shall respect the feelings and wishes of others. That does not mean you have to submit to them.
6. Thou shall look for the validity in the ideas of others. There is more than one way to look at things.
7. Thou shall apologize and make amends for your mistakes. Nothing will allow you to grow faster.
8. Thou shall want to forgive others for their mistakes, Do unto others as you would have them do unto you.
9. Thou shall not accept false apologies. They are worthless that no apologies at all.
10. Thou shall follow these commandments according to your best judgment. After all, they are not written in stone.

Top Tip

- Read one good book on the subject to understand the basics like Blink or working with emotional intelligence.
- Practice authentically expressing your feelings to your near and dear with an open agreement that they will share with you how your expression has impacted them and your relationship with them as a result.
- Attend some laboratory learning experiential workshop as may be suited to you at the right phase of life – it is better late than never.

Objectivity and Perception

It is believed that Mahatma Gandhi approved Jawaharlal Nehru for the Prime Minister's position of Independent India. Each country's President appoints various persons for various positions. The biggest Industrial House of India TATA appointed a non-family person as the successor for Mr.Ratan Tata, they have done so before also. If this suited any person observing the decision and the methodology that was followed, then that decision is said to be objective or else it is subjective. The Mahabharata is a demonstration of objectivity. A deeper look at the epic also depicts that leaders did play favorites in that epic too. So long as it was in the interest of overall righteous journey aligned with the big picture, it was considered objectivity. A deeper look at the reincarnation of god on earth in any manner be it Jesus or Krishna it took place with a subjective interest to make good prevail over the evil. The subjectivity is less here as the complete event is to uphold the good for the betterment of the universe. Objectivity is nothing but least subjectivity keeping overall bigger interest in mind not personal scores of the doer in context.

Behavioral Manifest of this Competency: Is all the time petty or personal likes and dislikes. Focuses all activities connecting to the overall interest to benefit system at large. Is able to present an open mind to situations as they unfold rising above or breaking the pet patterns of self level perceptions. Is able to strategically put ideas across to larger system to create congruence of thoughts.

Attitude	*Skill*	*Knowledge*
Wanting all the time to rise above petty needs and aligning and amending oneself to the big picture or cause. An attitude called open mind. Will of involving and evolving at right levels appropriately.	Skills to see the connecting overall picture. Constantly become aware of one's own personal barriers that hinder openness. Astute and perceptive communication skills with understanding of feedback and feed-forward.	Knowing what is right. Validating using all the resources as to right and wrong given a context. Wisdom to differentiate what is right in the overall interest rising above one's own personal likes and dislikes.

The other side of the coin could be – "objectivity is perception management". Any subject presented to a set of audience could go through the magic of individual perceptions and may not necessarily be in line or in same frequency of the message sending presenting person. In the Mahabharata Dhuryodana accused his guru dhronacharya of bias in favoring the Pandavas. The guru asked Dhuryodana to go on horse's back and identify few good persons in the city and come back. The student searched for the same and returned in the evening empty handed and said that he could not find any. He saw someone very honest and donating lots of wealth to poor people, but had the bad habit of drinking. He saw another person helping aged persons but was crazy to amass wealth for his family. Another person was very generous and helpful to destitute and orphans but was crazy about befriending his neighbor's wife. The search for good persons ended like this. The next day the guru sent the leader of the Pandavas on horse's back to identify some bad people and at end of the day he also returned empty handed. He saw the same sample of persons found that they were all good at something or other and in no way could he call any of them as bad.

The perception is often in the eye of the recipient as he/ she has ways of receiving, processing and responding to information and making one's own mental models about the perceived. The truth of the perceived object may be the same, the magic happens when goes through the human filter called individual perceptions. The way each one perceives could differ because of each perceiver's world of experiences both good and not so good. There is a possibility of the perceiver polluting the perceived. An astute corporate leadership role holder is aware of this fact and does manage perceptions of people at right stages of decision and implementation. The methodologies indulged in could be involvement of people at right level, making mass communication at right stage of decisions, using the grapevine effectively and enacting themselves right stage as a well managed stage drama, in other words, called premeditated/choreographed events. For example , an HR manager leaves a new policy draft on his table for two days. He obviously knows that some of his collegues will read it out of curiosity. Such readers, in turn, will talk amongst colleague about the formal new. The clever HR manager gets a feedback thus fine tunes the final version. This is one way of leveraging the grapevine.

A saint along with a disciple was crossing a river. While attempting to do so he found a helpless young woman wanting to cross over but scared and apprehensive seeing the flow of the river. The saint held the women across her in river crossing effort. After dropping her they were walking on their way to their shelter. The disciple asked the saint after about an hour, "Sir why did you being a saint hold the hands of a woman?". The saint replied, "I hold her hands for her safety for a few minutes and left, you still seem to be holding her hands".

Every leader's effort is to be appropriate to a given situation, we all are favorably inclined to some dimension during our decision making, . In other words we all have our preferences in making choices. "Are we doing so, for the sake of our personal likes or with a purpose aligned to the overall objective and the larger interest of the organization rather than personal likes only per-se" - is the essence of moving towards objective behavior in our role as leaders.

Top Tip

- Attempt to reflect on the day's transactions where you were able to maintain your objectivity - compare this with realities or perceptions that you have generated in others the next day.
- Ask to near and dear when they perceive you to be not objective or biased and compare the approach you have shown in this context with the point above - reflect what process corrections you could do in future.

Inclusiveness

"Inclusive leadership is about recognising and valuing diversity or difference, and valuing people, recognising them for their skills, experience and talent, and treating them equally and fairly - irrespective of their ethnic background, gender, age, sexual orientation, religion, belief, or of any disability they may have."

Morvia Gooden

The great leaders of the century Mahatma Gandhi, Martin Luther king, Gorbachev, Nelson Mandela, Mother Teresa and many others, all of them had one thing in common is that of taking every one along rather than identifying themselves with a particular group or ethnicity. They all may have fought/stood for a common cause; they never hurt or violently hit another group's interest.

Behavioral Manifest of this Competency: Transparently and openly relates to a cross section of people cutting across various sects, races, ethnicity, etc. Displays conduct in all deeds that he/she could relate one and all and could be related to by one and all. The underlying need to connect to others is always a common cause for society at large.		
Attitude	*Skill*	*Knowledge*
Respect for all individuals as equals and their value to bigger system. Love and respect for human kind cutting across race, ethnicity. Being humane	Constantly working on self to realize and appreciate love and respect for fellow citizens in a given environment.	Awareness of the truth that all are equals and unique in what they bring to the bigger system. No one had the right or control on the way they are born in particular race.

Good leaders by choice rise above particularistic fallacies or personalized likes and dislikes. They per-se believe in taking one and all, people around them together. They look at everyone as part of synergistic entity. Their guiding principle of life dominantly had remained 'love all'. In biblical language we are decedents of Adam and Eve, as in the Bhagvadgita we are belong to one family -"vasudeva kutumbakam". It means we have all evolved from the divine and in some way or other we are all related.

The simple thing that we all could relate to our real life story is that of what we do when our beloved daughter or son marries a person from some other sect of society. We resist to start with. If they persist, we accept with reluctance and over time we include them as integral part of us. Inclusion is all about how joyfully we enjoy this sense of belongingness to one and all around us. The best way to inculcate this habit is to recall how we were included when we were in an alien land at some part of our life. Many people who have made major shift in their life journey in terms of radically moving to some totally new location or field will have conviction on this subject. In simple terms this called exposure or becoming worldly wise.

Top Tip

- Draft a noble goal for yourself that you will like to leave behind for humanity, if you are not going to be around tomorrow. Read what it is that your mind urges you in this journey and the underlying principle. Could we practice it from today? (because tomorrow never comes).
- Listen, read or talk to someone who you think has come across to you like an inclusive leader, learn what has been their driving principle, to search for meaningful resonance for yourself.
- Read the philosophy of inclusiveness practiced by nations like US or Canada or Singapore and the process that they have adopted as a national mechanism(migration policy, land allotment or colonization of new land, etc). Draw what you could adopt from that model as a guiding principle.

Service Orientation

"A customer is not a problem, he is doing a favor by giving you an opportunity to serve him/her" by Mahatma Gandhi

Serve - Wise. This is the simplest and toughest definition of such a great topic that one could come across. The saint found a scorpion falling into a stream of water and struggling. He immediately used his hand and brought it to safety, during this process, the scorpion did strike him. After a while the scorpion again slipped and fell into water. The saint repeated his act of saving and so did the scorpion to strike him again. Some passerby noticed this and asked the saint why he was helping the scorpion when it was harming him. The saint replied, "It is doing its service; I am doing my service." If the scorpion is so determined in its service, he too should not give up. The theme in this story is important not the harm related in it.

Behavioral Manifest of this Competency: Is able to show sensitivity to customer needs with due sensitivity and empathy. Always behaves in line with ever changing expectations of the customer and considers that to be the foundation of business. Is relentless in raising the standard of service that he/she gives above what he/she takes from others.		
Attitude	*Skill*	*Knowledge*
Will to put customer beyond self all the time. Faith that the service standards are to be constantly raised before being demanded. Customer complaint is a gift and customer is the king and the person servicing the customer is the person giving idea about the organization to which he belongs (the organization is only as competent, knowledgeable, courteous, and reliable as the person who represents it).	Gathering information and sensing the context to identify the connectivity to the big picture in relation to the system that one belongs to.	Awareness that customer defines service. Knowing the ever changing standards of the customer requirement is the first step to achieving customer delight.

All of us have received service in many situations. We also provide service to others in many situations. Anything done using our bodily parts on occasions, supplemented by tools, to help another person for a particular purpose is a form of service. Since we are all service receivers we know what the definition of good quality service is. Reciprocally, when we provide service to others, we should use the same measuring rod as used while receiving. Thus, the level of service that we are used to getting becomes minimum level to be provided to others.

The true excellence in service orientation is all about how we can double our service levels. We expect a higher level of services as receivers but provide much less than that. This is called 'double standards' in service that is one for me and another for the others. Minimum service level should be equal to what we receive and expect when we are customers or service receivers. Achieving excellence model in service orientation is all about doubling our standards of service that we give to others than what we expect or receive when we are customers.

The author once did an exercise involving two groups of executives. The task of one group was to write in post-it slips the poor service that they had received in the recent past. The second group was to write the poor service delivery of theirs for which they were reprimanded by a boss or customer. When the groups compared the events, it was evident that each and every one was operating in double standards. What they were upset about reprimand for their genuine effort, for many appeared to be substandard service when they were service receivers in similar situations. For example, one person was very unhappy with the service that he/she got at a bank, because they took 14 minutes to make a draft. Same person noticed that the Boss had reprimanded him/her for failing to give receipt to a customer after four days of receiving the money. The person felt that the boss was very unreasonable in that reprimand. We often see our young generation getting upset when the fast food delivery person takes a little more time.

Essence of service excellence is that of differentiating what we do and how we do. This is the essence of difference that we experience when we go to have cup of tea. From a roadside restaurant, cafe or a posh hotel. All the places what is served could be tea the differentiating factor is all called service.

Bottom line - your customer is changing, double your service delivery standards or you may soon be out of business. Do not think that this only applies to organizations rather each individual is a service provider. What is the product? The 8 hours service in return for a pay cheque. If we do not constantly upgrade our service, we will be out of job.

Top Tip

- Identify some double standards that you have observed or practiced in your life either in the drawingroom or the boardroom.
- Identify, observe, and copy some service excellence model of your sort that you observe in someone who's service level that you would like to emulate as service delight model.
- Identify what has been the root cause of these double standards in your world of existence - what could you do to come out of the same (take the help of your mentor in finding answer to this question).
- Revisit your CV (your product brochure) every periodicity (once in twelve/six months) and see has your product brochure been upgraded significantly for the service receiver to continue with you.

Negotiating for Win-Win

I win you lose
You win I lose
Both of us win
Which is better?

A poor man passed away leaving behind an expensive shawl, a cow and a small hut. This was inherited by his two sons. The elder son negotiated with the younger brother that the house and shawl will belong to him during the night and cow's rear part. The rest of the day time those assets will belong to the younger brother and the front part of the cow all the time to the younger brother. As days passed by he used the house to sleep in the night and used the shawl to cover himself during winters and of course milked the cow at appropriate time and used the cow dung as manure for agriculture. The younger brother had nothing for himself functional, contrary he had to the feed the cow when she made noise with hunger. He got wise counsel from a friend. He could wet the shawl in the day time as it belonged to him and throw lots of water into the house everywhere in the evening. Whenever the elder brother was milking the cow he started beating the cow on its face. The elder brother realized the reality and now came down to fair negotiation for a win-win. In essence a good negotiation is one in which both parties are winners. If one party alone benefits, it would be a short-lived honeymoon. The losing party will wait to hit back and the process would become unpleasant and counter-productive to both the parties.

Behavioral Manifest of this Competency: Is clear in differentiating various negotiating situations and aligns behavior conducive to that same. Is facilitative of negotiating processes leading to sustained win-win for parties involved, with intent to build long-term mutually flourishing relationships.

Attitude	*Skill*	*Knowledge*
Willingness to search a win-win for all concerned. Faith that together the pie could always be enhanced.	Data interpretation, looking the current and possible related outcome for each. Enhancing the pie.	Awareness that for sustained relationship both parties should have some benefit commensurate with efforts.

Good negotiation is all about planning and knowing what is the interest of both the parties, rather than only focusing on what is in it for me.

What is the core competence of each party and how much of it could be leveraged by the other party without any loss to the provider?

Is this a long term relationship or purely one off situation? In that case what is the value or self image that I want to live and leave behind in the mind of the other party?

Once a company was putting up a new plant in a remote village location. The organization decided to provide plentiful unlimited food to its employees in the canteen and the canteen operation was outsourced to a professional contractor. The contractor was asked to give a quotation for his food providing services. The manager who was negotiating did his homework and found out that X would be the cost per plate as per the prevailing rates of the ingredients in the market + labor costs, etc. When both parties reached the negotiating table the contractor quoted 63% of X much to the surprise of the negotiating manager. They signed off an annual contract for this amount/rate and the work began. In about 15 days

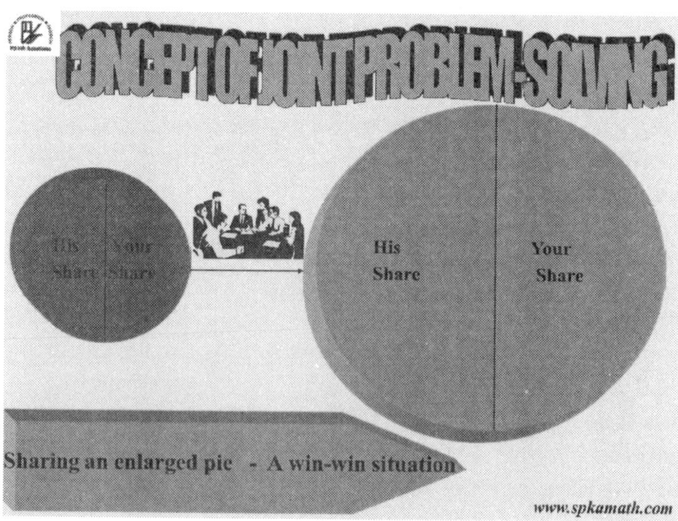

of the work commencement the contractor ran away without informing the manager. The operation came to a standstill leading to labor unrest. Later on the manager had to sign up the next contractor at 127% of X and start work on a fast forward basis. Planning should be in the interest of the both the parties. The truth is that the contractor does exist to provide service and also make some profit.

Both the parties also plan to see what is immediate and what is in store for long term such that the overall size of the pie/cake could be enlarged over time in their best of interest. For example, when the sub-prime crisis was on, there was dip in business for many persons. An organization (which works in an industrial area where Saturday and Sunday are working days with Friday as weekly off) negotiated with a service provider to visit them at 70% of his fee on Saturdays and Sundays. Hence, the service provider agreed to drop the fee after negotiations. The organization got price decreased, the service provider got a deal signed for 24 months, each month Saturday and Sunday. Both got their pie enlarged. Can each party be one another's goodwill ambassadors? Some effort is required on the part of parties to discover the opportunities to enlarge the pie. The truth is very many occasions the opportunity would exist in a blatant or hidden manner.

Top Tip

- Relate to some of personal life negotiations done by you which has lasted the test of time. Identify the underlying principles and processes. Specific to trust levels, overall benefit derived by both parties in short run and long run.
- Learn from a case of failed negotiation - about the type of deal breakers that crept in that you were unprepared the values that each other party violated. This could be learnt from other professionals also if you have not been a party to such work.

Strategic Thinking and Business Savvy

A shoe sales person goes to a village and finds nobody using shoes and comes back with the conclusion, there is no market for shoes. Another person finds the same place with immense potential for shoes sales. Seeing the unseen is what a strategy is all about. Having seen the unseen opportunity, all that the shoe man does to help people buy shoes is all about executing strategy.

A person who is in the business of lending household furniture on hire always reads classified advertisement column in newspaper page on house rental required. The objective is to call such needy persons to explore - do they also need furniture on hire.

Behavioral Manifest of this Competency: All the time looks beyond the obvious. Senses the related factors in the environment around, involves related persons and evolves with a long-term path to glory. Takes mid course stock/ reviews from time to time such as to align/amend as may be necessary. Has the knack of identifying business opportunity other than the or beyond the obvious.		
Attitude	*Skill*	*Knowledge*
Urge to walk on the path unwalked or less walked to gain productively. Seeing the hidden beyond the obvious.	Scanning the environment. Data interpretation Sensing larger issues	Sourcing of information, knowing competition present and emerging/hidden.

Guts to take calculated risk. Will to deal with the unknown variables. Flexible attitude, Inclusiveness as regards implications of decisions.	involved with long time perspective.	

A merchant had three of his loyalists employed with him for long. All the three were being paid differentially despite having got same experience. One day the less paid two persons raised the issue of this pay disparity. The merchant without any explanation gave them all a task of inspecting the newly arrived salt dispatch at the yard where there were lots of rains.

Person one came back and reported the exact truth with complete accuracy at the fastest time possible.

The second person came with the information but had taken the initiative to cover the stocks with some water proof cover, etc., and safeguarded the material on his own initiative.

Knowing the cost effectiveness of such a value added activity, he also had found some details of best term of offer of insurance cover available in the market.

The third person had spoken to nearby town people where there was no rain and the market was selling well without any rain related sluggishness. Came to the merchant with the data and the likely profit that they can make by disposing of the stocks as is where is to a trader at the next town at a particular price, sought his approval.

Obviously the third person was the highly paid employee amongst the loyalists.

The word strategy is most intimidating to many people. A simplistic view is that what one does to overcome competition or be ahead of competition. In other words what is that we do to differentiate ourselves from the rest of the herd? If this is done reactively it is termed firefighting, if done proactively it is called strategy. A strategy maker takes a little time to think ahead to save time later. The old cave man also had a cutting edge when he had the longest rod. The colonial British Empire had the guns when the world was fighting with swords. So did the advanced nations have nuclear arsenal before the rest of the world could get that technology. It is all about the cutting edge over the others.

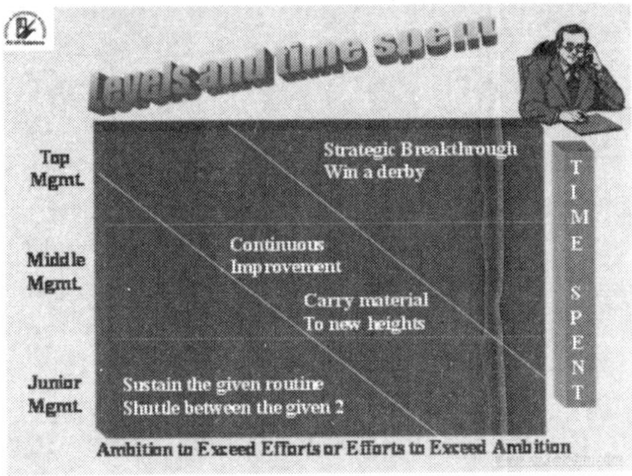

A donkey shuttles with baggage from the washerman's house to the pond where the washerman goes for washing. He lets the donkey for grassing. That is all the reward the donkey gets for such contribution. Junior management persons get paid less than other seniors, because they spend 70 percent time in routine work, 25 percent time in making improvements and only 5 percent in contributing towards breakthrough results. The above picture depicts three segments for the Junior person in that ratio of 70 : 20 : 10.

A mule takes material to higher altitudes or pilgrims up the hills. At the end of the day when the owner gets paid for the service, he does feed the mule with some good food and water + pats the mule for the earnings. That is the reward such act earns. The middle management person gets relatively well paid because he/she spends 10 percent of the time in handling the escalated routine issues from the juniors, 70 percent time in doing continuous improvements to make things better and 10 percent time in complementing breakthrough decisions. His ratio is 10 : 70 : 10.

A Derby winning horse wins a couple of Derbies in life time; the owner celebrates and takes utmost care of the horse.

In our thinking and contributions when we give that kind of cutting edge to our organization we become valued Derby winning horses and get treated valuably. That is what individual brand building is all about through strategic thinking. This is what is expected from the top management involved in management committee to invest 70% time in strategic breakthrough decision making processes, 10 percent time in managing and encouraging improvement and 10% time in overseeing routines.

Sports persons with high advertisement revenue earning are one such example in their area of expertise. They have a cutting edge over the rest. We all need to take a stock how our eight hours of time in the organization are invested and in what activities, the rewards and recognition will automatically follow.

Every time a door closes another opens. The person with business acumen is always ahead to see the door that is opening rather than getting bogged down by the door that is closing. There are people in the world consuming and surviving all the time, the location where it is flourishing and happening and where it is truncated could be different at times. All people around/business around are not closing down during adversity, they are finding some way to sail forward. Can we have that outlook to find our way? The recent sub-prime crisis in US that triggered worldwide concerns also threw up opportunities for many other economies. Some bad debt managing firms flourished during this time. Some other consuming economies flourished. Some economies spent spare time building people competencies for the future and to be ready up there.

Top Tip

- See persons who are your contemporaries and are way ahead in career. Note what they had done in their capability building three years back when you were at the same level.

- Look at the typical time log of a highly successful person in terms of time spent in routines task execution and thinking ahead.
- One can read good books on this subject like the *Blue Ocean Strategy, Mission Possible* or *Good to Great*. What initiatives differentiate the successful from the herd around?
- Throw yourself to some unknown situation without any resources in hand, see what thoughts and processes you could indulge in building your resources

Quality Consciousness

"Over commit under Perform
Commitment = Delivery
Under commit over Perform"

Quality is a habit or an obsession - If you do not demand quality and settle for substandard things, you will continue to get substandard things. Any time there is a difference in what we deliver as against what we commit to our customer we have slipped up in quality. The game that we play using any of the other two terms we mentioned above is a short lived concept of quality.

Quality is what your customer specifies. In other words quality is meeting customer's specifications and the customer has the right to change the specifications. In the initial stages of six sigma revolutions, a Japanese company got an order from abroad to supply some components at six sigma level. When they asked what the six sigma levels were, the buyer company explained that there could only be possibility of

3.4 errors in a million components supplied to them. The Japanese company promptly supplied a million quality components meeting the specification of the customer and separately packed 3.44 erroneous components and shipped the consignment. Since they did not appreciate the concept of error in manufacturing and also did not know what the customer meant by such a specification, they promptly complied with the customer specification. Japanese manufacturers take pride process as they believe strongly that quality is manufactured and not checked. They talk all the time total quality and zero defect in their manufacturing processes and service levels.

The simplest definition of quality is fitting customer specifications all the time on time, in turn, generating customer satisfaction. It is all about creating customer delight.

Behavioral Manifest of this Competency: Is all the time respectful of what the customer specifies as requirement. Puts in all efforts and techniques to meet and beat those expectations. Takes pride that quality is produced not checked.

Attitude	*Skill*	*Knowledge*
Respect for ever changing customer specifications. "Doing it right the first time every time" attitude.	Quality orientation in all the acts (total quality processes). Ability to monitor and calibrate processes up to date to churn out consistent quality.	Awareness that quality sells and delighted/ satisfied customer becomes the ambassador for further sale.

The concept of quality originates from human beings who are called Total Quality Persons. Such persons believe and take pride in giving quality in all that they do.

Such people design Total Quality Processes and ensure that whatever they indulge in is quality, in other words all the time meet all the customer specifications or beat the customer specification.

The above two evolves from and around Total Employee Involvement. That means people involved in the processes are respected that each person doing a work knows the work the most. His/her total involvement is key for the above two to happen with consistency.

A Honda motor assembly employee who assembles wiper blades in the car finishes his shift and goes home. While on his way home in case he finds any Honda car parked with wiper blade not correctly aligned, he stops and corrects their setting and proceeds. The obsession is to see the wiper assembly to perfection is his way of life. The examples about Japan as a country or Japanese organizations in terms of quality is synonymous, because it is a country at large obsessed with quality. We have lots to learn from the attitude that nation carries in this subject without a debate.

Top Tip

- Try to give quality to your family members and see how it influences your relationships.
- Try listening to your customer's language as to what he/she specifies or perceives as quality.

Motivating and Developing Self and Others

Whether you think you Can, Or think you Can't, You're right."

Henry Ford (On Self Motivation)

"Motivation is the art of getting people to do what you want them to do because they want to do it."

Dwight D. Eisenhower (On Motivating Others)

A few centuries back in a small village there were three persons involved in the labor of breaking marble stones into a particular shape and size. A stranger passerby asked the first person – "What are you doing?" – The man replied, "Can't you see I am breaking marbles in a particular shape as instructed by my boss." The stranger asked the same question to the second person, he replied "Sir, I am breaking marbles for the construction of an important monument that is going to be constructed in the nearby site". The stranger asked the same question to the third person, he said, "Sir I am in the process of making a great monument to be called Taj Mahal in memory of our late empress Mumtaj Begam, this is likely to be revered by one and all in times to come as world wonder."

Behavioral Manifest of this Competency: Releases energy unconditionally to make things happen. Draws lots of energy from within because of positive belief and faith in what he/she does. Involves people around and encourages them on all the positivity's that they bring to the team.

Attitude	*Skill*	*Knowledge*
Enjoying what one is doing and doing exactly what one enjoys. Being passionate to one's professional pursuit.	Seeking purpose, clarifying the objective for a particular act or abstinence before doing, skills in choosing things which are to the liking of the person or want enhancing acts.	Awareness to one's own likings. Need to choose the profession which is close to one's heart. Need to say no for things that do not positively suit one's likes.

A king called one of his brilliant scientists and asked him to make out whether the new crown made by his goldsmith is of pure gold and the weight specified by the maker is correct. He also warned the scientist that he cannot tamper with the crown in finding this truth, if he does not verify and confirm this truth in a given number of days he will behead the scientist. The baffled scientist was restless and sleepless next few days by this king's order, in his bathtub he found the answer for this question and screamed "Eureka". There came the invention of the Archimedes principle. A few months later Rome was to invade Greece, this time the baffled Greece king called the same scientist and praised him a lot with folded hands, requested him to save the kingdom from the invasion of the other emperor. As the ships were sailing towards the Greece Empire in the Mediterranean Sea and the time was limited, the scientist this time used his innovative sense and used lenses to converge the sunlight and reflect the powerful concentrated hot sunlight towards the sails of the ships in the high seas. As the sails got burnt, the ships could not reach and invade their target, the battle was won by the emperor at the high seas itself.

Whilst the first incident is that of negative or fear motivation and the second one is that of positive motivation. The fact is both work, where to use and when to use what is a judgment call that the user has to take.

Another twin concept about motivation is that of motivation from within and motivation from outside. When a person derives motivation from within he / she becomes a self start engine and is charged up all the time. When a person derives motivation from outside, it has a linkage to that source and becomes often a dependent variable. A clever manager is one who facilitates the person to discover his/her source of motivation.

If a person could choose an activity, that resonates with his/her values and passion, he or she will never have a day's work to do. Motivation is unconditional release of energy towards work directed behavior and being joyful about it. In other words, feeling the joy of going to work and not being pained by the need to go to work. When one is not at work such a joy is not experienced or such a joy is getting reduced, it is time for the person to take it up for changing the role or seeking help. Hesitating to deal with such a situation is lose-lose for all the parties involved in the context.

There was a part-time professor for an executive MBA programme. As he has been doing this work for some time he developed some relationships. One day when he was travelling to a particular city an old student met with him on his way and started chatting. The student wanted guidance from him as to how to quit his job and start on his own work. The professor said, "Please find answers to three of my questions. We will discuss it further once you answer these questions."

1. What is your passion that you are willing to work unconditionally?
2. What are the personal values that you will never compromise in your life?
3. What are the disciplines in which you have professional core competence that you can deliver superior results at any point in time any where?

The student assured that he would get back next day with answers for discussions and they could take it forward. The next evening the student called up Prof and said, "sir these are very tough questions I need few months to get back to you". After a few months he found a self-employed vocation that was in line with the three above question in positive sense. He is now a successful practitioner in this vocation.

Motivation is all from within and to be motivated about something you need to align passion, personal values and professional competence. When a person chooses such job or vocation, he/she will never have a day's work to do. The author often goes for adventure sports (like rafting rappelling) to conduct outbound team building workshops. Many people say we all pay to enjoy this adventure sports, you get paid to enjoy the same with us as faculty. That is the secret to motivation. Many of us get involved into acts because they are well paying, they are flashy, they are visible, they are good in looks and facilities, etc., these things cease to be a motivator when we lose the charm or when we get used to it over time. That is why secret to motivation is all about marrying passion to profession and person's values.

Foundation to Motivation

Certain – Questions ???	Truth - Answers
• Am I a good soul	• I am a good soul
• Have I achieved my best	• My best is yet to come
• Can I make a difference	• I Do make a difference
• Am I comparable	• I am unique
• Who is in -charge of me	• I am in -charge myself
• Do I doubt my beliefs	• What else I can trust
• Why always me	• All happens for good

All the above questions, all the time answered from within by a person and a leader making people believe in them is all about in affirmative is the essence of motivating self and motivating others. The question as to then what leaders do to motivate others.

They enable each person to see the hidden potential.

They involve people in subject that matters to them.

They demonstrate in their conduct self belief that inspires their juniors.

They call out when the person deviates in negative direction.

They identify with skill of positive self talk and enable others to do it with care, concern and compassion.

Top Tip

- Invest some time to find out what is it that you can do for 14 hours a day without feeling tired. This is likely to be your passion. Ask someone who knows you better to help you identify this answer.
- Apart from your formal qualification identify your core competence that you can deliver superior results consistently with relative comfort and least effort.
- What are your strict dos and don'ts of life or your life guiding principles that you will never compromise on.
- Is there any work or vocation that without any conflict aligns with the above three points - seek a guru's help to find such a field. Take time to find this, never be in a hurry to identify this field.

Leadership

The art and science of enhancing the 'Want To Do' attitude in people given a group objective is what leadership is all about and any person who does this is a leadership role holder.

Behavioral Manifest of this Competency: Is focused on the main objective driven conduct in self and one and all, shows the willingness to let go his/her leader's role to the 'leadership/direction providing person' on all occasions when he finds opportunity to leverage synergies for the betterment of the team. Demonstrates the values that he professes, never relents in taking decisions as situations call for.

Attitude	*Skill*	*Knowledge*
Mutual respect for one another's resources (time, money, efforts).	Personal organization and ability to prioritize. Ability to involve other people. Ability to communicate effectively.	Awareness that time, money and efforts are valuable resources. Become aware of priorities in life and related way of putting them to use.

Leader is a person appointed to hold a role given certain objective and leadership is a dynamic role that moves from one person to another, given a situation. In a game of cricket, when the ball is tossed to a bowler the leadership shifts to the bowler, though the captain continues to be the appointed leader. A good leader is all the time able to see the difference and conduct himself accordingly. Another example could be when a country is at war with another nation, the president could continue to be the elected leader but the leadership automatically shifts to the general of the armed forces. If the president is sensitive to leave the right decisions to the specialist and play his political leader's role effectively he would be called an effective leader. In Indian history, Gandhiji and Nehru, Chanakya and Chandragupta maurya, in many nations the President and Prime Minister-in all these cases the leader holds the role but becomes a follower par excellence when it comes to respecting leadership. Many managers who hold leadership roles struggle to recognize the importance of their followership styles to leadership situations, more so when the mantle passes on to them legitimately.

The other way around an example - at a four road meeting road number 4 leading to the best hospital and the situation is as follows:

Road 1: The presidential motorcade is moving as the president wants to visit the hospital for a routine health check up.

Road 2: An ambulance is rushing with a patient on emergency to be taken to the hospital.

Road 3: A fire brigade vehicle is on emergency call to the hospital as there is fire in the emergency ward.

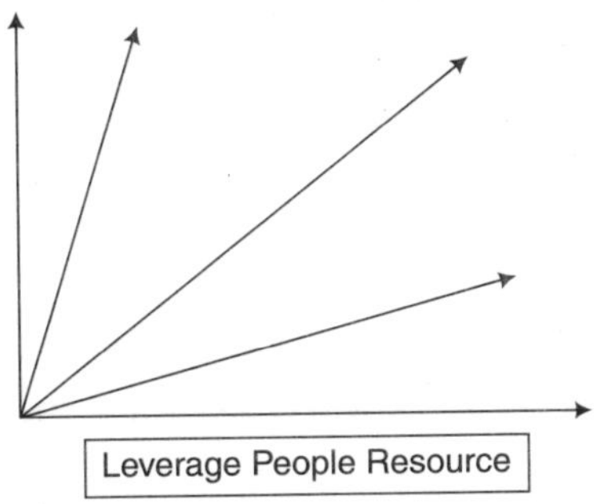

The leader of the country could still be the president but the leadership to decide priority as to which vehicle to be permitted to move on road four first is left with the traffic police regulating the traffic. Some people call it functional authority. Good leaders are clever enough to recognize and leverage leadership flow rather than be fixated about their position that they hold.

Essential ingredients of leadership to be remembered by all practitioners are:

- Accepting that there is no one specific definition which exists for leadership.
- It is purely contextual or situational and never a case of one measure fits all.
- Leadership is more valuable for a leader than per se the leader focus all the time.
- Leaders are both born and made.

- Whilst leverage caringly all resources (like people, material, money) and focus on achieving tasks, they do take decision as important facilitating processes.

Top Tip

- Worth it to read some applied research books on the subject as there are plenty available in the market. Watch the kind of leadership style shown by a same person in two different situations of success.
- Watch out from epics cutting across religion, what is.
- What is the importance of envisioning and value based approach to long-term leadership role.
- Read a good book of applied research on leadership like good to great or Built to last.

Communication

"Communication is what a receiver understands"

There was an advertisement in the daily newspaper for filling up an urgent position of a security officer with a company on a given day. That evening there was theft in that company's premise. Did the communication work? The advertisement which was intended to attract the eyes of the prospective security officer candidates also attracted the attention of thieves. Here the communication worked much more than the required level of the audience.

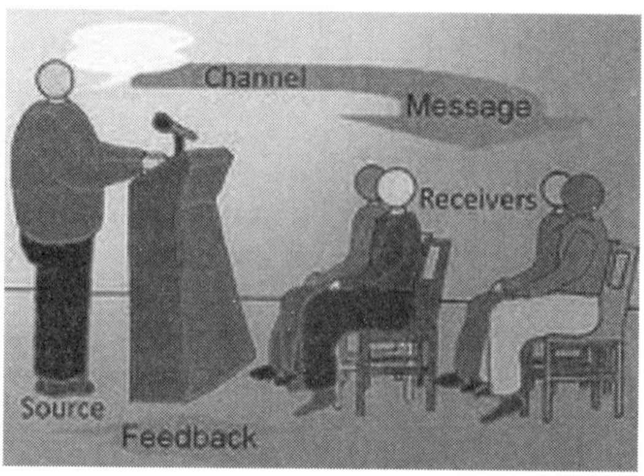

Behavioral Manifest of this Competency: Is very sensitive to the understanding capability of the receiver of the message in context, gets the message across in the simplest possible way with complementing body expressions and tone befitting the message. Does close the loop of message as to the receiver's perception by seeking feedback all the time.		
Attitude	*Skill*	*Knowledge*
Never takes communication for granted. Believes there could always be a slip up and ensures to tally the receiver's end understanding is the intent.	Thought clarity. Message brevity. Receiver sensitivity. Ability to choose and leverage the appropriate medium and tools.   	Awareness that communication creates perceptions and managing the same is integral part of managerial life.

90/10 Principles of Communication

Brevity/Precision/ Comprehension	long winding/articulation
Expression	Impression
Simplicity	Complexity
Effectiveness	Efficiency
How (process sensitivity)	What (content obsession)
Quality	Quantity

Elements of effective communication are:

Leveraging the tools

Remembering the 90/10 principles

Closing the loop

Remaining sensitive and relevant to a context

Conceptual clarity and contextual congruence

In essence, communication is all about saying what you mean and meaning what you want to say in your messages. Doing it all the time with consistency, in turn, creating understanding in the audience would be a delight.

Top Tip

- Listen to often (maximum strikes/viewership) watched video clips in YouTube and see how the above principles are applied.
- Listen to the speech or writings or e-mails of great leaders to identify how they have applied 90/10 of communication philosophies.

Team Working

"Together each achieves more"

Migratory birds fly across thousands of kilometers during the change of season. Whilst none of them has the capacity to fly that long alone, together all of them leverage the air passage made by first bird and rest fly using only 30% of their energy. They change the leader's role with passage of some distance and together cover a long distance. Many of us may have witnessed the V shape of flying birds in the sky, the first bird alone is doing the trick of 100% energy and cutting the air passage of the rest to leverage at 30% efficiency. The jargon world calls it synergy.

Universal survey findings reveal when questioned on a subject. In case there is a choice to save only either the mother or child to be born – most have responded the mother. The logics emerged were simple:

(a) The mother is a known existing relationship.
(b) If the mother exists she can have another baby.
(c) Without the mother who will feed and nurture the baby.

Team working is all about this when team interest is at question. For this all the time the members must be clear as to which decision is the mother. In team working language it is called seeing the big picture and aligning with the same. The secret to achieve better team working is always have plenty of open communication amongst the members, throwing away the personal bias or and making amends in each one's conduct to align with the big picture. A good leadership role player is always able to see the big picture and enable others to see the same in resolving issues whilst working together.

The powerful word in English that describes the phenomenon is called synergy.

Behavioral Manifest of this Competency: Respects interdependence as truth when working others. Is able to see and identify with the big picture the overall interest of the group and align own behavior to become subordinate to the overall goal, making shifts from the stands that he/ she has taken.		
Attitude	*Skill*	*Knowledge*
Will to become subservient to the bigger goal or overall interest sacrificing self level or self centered interests.	Knack of identifying with the big picture. Skill to reach out to one another and reason out issues with openness.	Knowing that the overall interest is above individual stand points.

In organizations we are all bound to work with more than one person in any function. It could be part of a department in coordination with others even at individual capacity. Hence, team working is an imperative for all of us in our life's journey.

Certain basic elements of team working are as follows:

- Mutual trust.
- Common shared goal amongst the members of the team.
- Open flow of communication without formal barriers amongst team members.
- Appreciation for truth called synergy
- Appreciation for truth called interdependence.
- Will to explore interpersonal differences with a clarity which is in the overall interest.
- All forces in the team to become subordinate to bottleneck point immaterial of the power vested with

other processes. For example, if a person's operated right leg has the capacity to run only five km the other leg's excess capacity to run 10 km has now to become subordinate to the right leg. The entire efficiency of the bottle is that of the operating speed of the neck, other parts have to facilitate this speed.

Some fundamental operating guidelines to be remembered whilst working in teams are:

- Championship for the team is a must, enroute the journey if someone achieves man of the match it is welcome.
- In any dilemma situation or limited choice between 2 options always save the mother rather than the child. It means overall interest or global excellence is more important than local excellence.
- Over communicate rather than less communication.
- Identify the bottleneck and see that all forces contribute their excess capacity in supporting the bottleneck operation to function 100%.

Top Tip

- Observe and learn from the consistently performing teams as to what are methods they use in addressing the above aspects of working.
- See what big leaders do in selling their conceptualized overall objective to the rest of the team members and when they do.
- Experiment in your comfort zone of team working to identify which is the bottleneck operation. For example, in a picnic, knowing who is the special person or slowest person, now making each member do something to help this person during the entire picnic. Now translate this experience in other walks of world.

Change

"Change is the only constant and resistance to change is another constant"

"Are you part of the change that you want bring about," asked Gandhiji. During the Second World War there used to be three persons who accompany the cannons. One person was to carry the ammunition and feed it. The second person's duty was to operate the cannon, the third person's duty was to hold the horse that was used for dragging the cannon as it would hump when was fired. After the war lots of cannons became motorized, etc., still the three positions continued.

We all post our own three cannon carriers in our lives. Our own cannons have been motorized with laptops, mobiles and other gadgets but still we at times continue to post 3 carriers and do not revisit what has changed. When we say let us watch for some more time, the reason is our internal resistance to change.

Behavioral Manifest of this Competency: A willing person, who trusts that change is way of life, loves to embrace change with lots of openness. Is willing to try out new things and see how they align with emerging situations of the day and near future given overall scheme of things. Enjoys being part of creating and driving change in work situations.

Attitude	*Skill*	*Knowledge*
Belief that change is constant and inevitable. Will to try out newer things. Openness Infusing change rather than coping with it.	Trying newer things and seeing the opportunities that such effort throws up.	Awareness that aligning with change is advantageous in long run. Need is to rough out with changing conditions.

If we ask a question-"what has not changed in life?" The reply will be emphatic nothing. Scientifically, it is a proven truth that in the human body there are trillion transactions of cells taking place every second. That is the speed of change bestowed by nature. In other words there is nothing that is not changing. Yet we are all so uncomfortable about change. The simplest way to understand is that if we do not embrace change, we will be left behind. Yesteryear's typewriters were integral part of an organization to write anything legible. In the modern era when computers invaded the corporate world, those typists who did not change themselves to become computer operators became jobless. This is the truth with any change that has invaded the world. The choice of each person is:

- To be part of the change and change.
- Foresee such change and proactively prepare oneself and be ahead of the herd or resist such a change and become extinct.

The highest level of this state of being is to introduce change ourselves ahead of others. In other words leaders induce change and facilitate others to adopt and implement change.

Top Tip

- Try to change the room layout of your living room every month and experience.

- Try to change the way you arrange your wardrobe each quarter and see how it helps.
- Change the way you organize your folders in the e-mail box once in a quarter and see how it helps your personal organization and functionality.

Innovation and Creativity

"When we all think alike than no one is thinking"

A French engineer was involved in the construction of narrow gauge railway line through the hilly terrain of Darjeeling, the beautiful hill station in Himalayas - India. At a point in the track construction, he encountered a steep climb and the work could not proceed any further as it was technically impossible to go that steep in terms of laying railway track. Of course he was upset and puzzled with this challenge. His wife called him and asked why he could not come and go. His intuition said this sentence of his wife had a solution. After a few days of incubation all he did was to take the track diagonally to a point again return and do the same to achieve eventually the height. He got it.

Many solutions to problems that we encounter are hidden around us. It is our resilience to uncover those hidden diamonds and take things forward. Are we creative enough to see those situations or do we resign ourselves to fate?

Behavioral Manifest of this Competency: Believes firmly that there is always a better way of doing things. Given so many changes around that seem to be constant, there is a reason for each are of our work to innovate a better way than the present way of doing things.

Attitude	*Skill*	*Knowledge*
High will to explore the unknown. Grit to experiment limitlessly for bettering the best.	Risk taking and active experimentation. Resilience and working with stretching conditions.	Knowing that there is always a better way, Innovation is key to future Innovation provides cutting edge for all strategic initiatives.

Creativity is all about ideation for creating what does not exist and innovation is implementation of such ideas or about putting such ideas to functional use for the real world of our utility. Creativity is thinking process and innovation is productive process. Creativity is mother of innovation. As one follows the other these terms are always used together and no need to nitpick on them. It is all about being uncomfortable about a road block and relentlessly see things around to discover the hidden paths. Contextually all people around the subject could have some ideas, all we need is an open mind to listen and incubate the ideas and see how we could take any of them forward to a workable solution.

$$5 + 5 + 5 = 550$$

Could you make the above equation by using one (1) only once?

Yes there are many ways to do it.

545 + 5 = 550 (putting slanting line as 1 in the first plus making it 4 that makes the equation look 545 + 5).

5 + 545 = 550 (putting slanting line as 1 in the second plus making it 4 and results the equation to read 5 + 545).

5 + 5 + 5 # 550 (here we are talking about not equal to).

– = 550 score this off with a long horizontal one. We score off our wrong writing – don't we?

The above are some methods that we are aware of, but our set mind or mind set is the limitation. All innovators of the electric bulb, MS Office various versions, e-mails system, face book, high fuel efficient engine technologies, mission to moon, etc., never gave up when they failed. When the landlines existed in telephony, inventors went for pagers, they failed, cell phones succeeded. They looked at risk and failures en route that process as an opportunity for further progress. The urge of wanting to see the unseen and the zeal to explore the unknown is the attitude that is required to make a commencement in this process. Columbus or Vasco da Gama precisely demonstrated this quality to explore and for them the globe was the limit. Not alone they did accomplish something, they could also inspire others to explore.

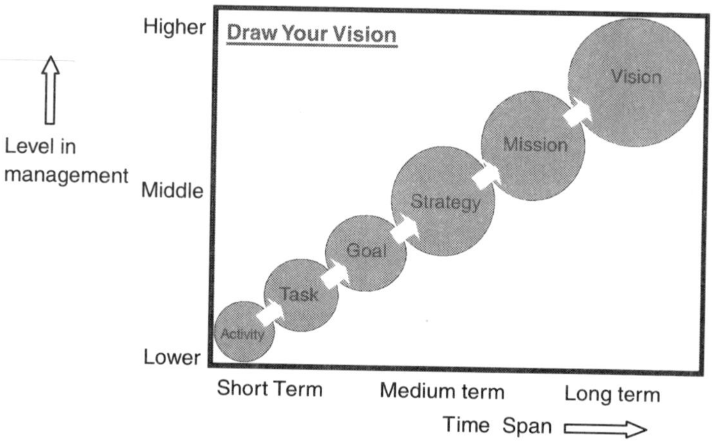

In all this we are trying to explore different methods that will give us a better way provided we are willing to experiment and explore newer dimensions. The easy experiment at this level would eventually give us an attitude of 'the will to explore the unknown' at a very high level too.

- In the above diagram a person at a junior level is expected to comply with activities and tasks on a day to day basis or weekly basis.
- The next level is that of a middle level person who is supposed to involve his junior during spare time and evolve innovative ideas to make improvements in the way we do tasks such that the monthly or yearly target improvements are achieved to provide cutting edge to the organization.

- The third level is that of the top management, who are all the time using available environmental innovative opportunities and see the unseen. In turn, they are expected to leverage all their resources to provide a breakthrough for the organization that will give a quantum leap in the society that they exist in.

Higher you grow, this competency of creativity and innovation becomes a critical requirement for job success at senior levels. This is not so only in organizational life, it is even applicable in personal life. Either you have this quality or have the appreciation for this quality where ever it flows from, assuming you are quick to adopt and leverage the same. Thinking that this is someone else's job would become a handicap.

Top Tip

- Can we drive back to and fro to our work place through different routes rather than the beaten track of same route?
- Can we go for morning walk through different routes rather than repeated track?
- Could we experiment our dressing processes, cooking processes, house maintenance processes with untried methods?

Mentoring and Coaching – People Development

Certain intensive skills based vocational jobs like tyre repair does not have technical training courses in the Indian sub-continent. Is also a fact there is industry need for these skilled personnel. Where do these technically skilled persons originate?

A deeper look at the tyre repair job reveals that all these vocations are practiced in road side small shops headed by a skilled person called the "Ustad" who, in turn, has a few junior helpers popularly called "Chotu". The chotu is normally a needy person, who has been hired by the ustad for his miscellaneous help. Over time this chotu migrates from small jobs of opening the tyre, taking out the tube, spotting the punctured spot, getting tea, etc., for the senior to higher quality job of fixing punctured tube, etc. Once the chotu picks up skills he opens up his own shot and hires some juniors.

Now this could be extrapolated to many other vocations like truck driving, mechanical jobs in workshops, buffing and painting/white washing. The list of such vocations goes long. This skill building that happens is all about mentoring and coaching in our sophisticated management language.

Behavioral Manifest of Competency: **Mentoring and Coaching** – Believes in the joy of giving and enabling others. Trusts enabling and empowering people with skills and sharpening their ownership of certain attitudes will enhance their competency. Loves to question and challenge the existing paradigms of people, trusts in others potential, urge and uptake that will make them learn. Does not believe in spoon feeding instead nurtures self realization and evolution with iterative experiential processes. Willingly creates experiences for people and patiently enables them to internal realize for changed behavior.

Attitude	*Skill*	*Knowledge*
Will to wait for self evolutions to emerge. Will to let go. Restraint on urge to spoon feed. Faith each person has the capacity to work and evolve given the experiences. Joy of giving a craft.	Observation Facilitative Questioning Patience Countering dependency needs.	Knowing that people have immense potential to learn and grow. Awareness of various types of questioning and need to create adults to gain their own experiences to comprehend things better as against lecturing and sermonizing.

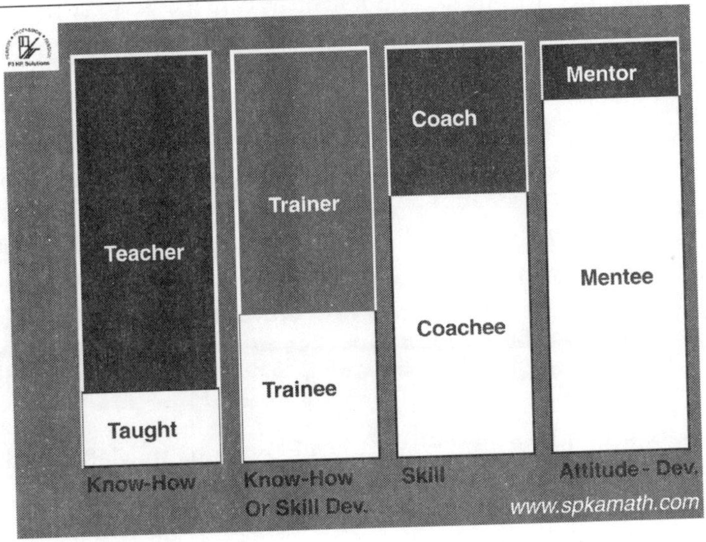

The above picture is a simple depiction of various levels of enabling people to learn. One may observe the bar being shaded differently. This depicts the involvement on the part of provider and the receiver.

- In classroom of schools the teacher lectures about 80% time and the students at best are involved talking doing things to 20% extent. This has been the pattern of classroom teaching for long. Predominantly instructional method. The first bar diagram depicts this state.
- The second bar diagram represents situation of typical trainer and trainee involvement ratio in a training room of a corporate which happens to be 60 : 40 of trainer trainee involvement. Any programme that went too much of lecture would have taken it back to previous step of school teaching.
- Bar diagram three symbolizes the work of tennis coach or swimming coach to coachee the ratio of active involvement changes now the other way around to 40 : 60. Dronacharya to Arjun in Mahabharata was coaching. The coach also had expertise in the skill called

archery. Any skill we learnt in our life would reaffirm this process may be we learnt a musical instrument or a sporting skill. This is a structured pairing done by parents with a coach with a wish to make the coachee imbibe a particular skill. This relationship often runs into a longer tenure but certainly would have an end when the coachee acquires sufficient levels of the requisite skill.

- The fourth bar diagram presents the relationship of mentor to mentee. As we talk about the mentoring situation the mentor's involvement and work is as low as 20% and it is by and large mentee driven to 80% extent.
- Krishna to Arjun, Shakuni to Duyodana in Mahabharata in the battle royal is a classic case of mentoring.
- In both the cases the mentee chose the mentor.
- Another truth was that the mentor did not specialize in the skill of relevance. All the mentor did was challenging mentee's way of thinking; it is the mentee who went on to achieve the goal. All the time the mentee had a doubt or a question the mentor replied the same with a question, never gave an answer. The mentor believed the mentee has it in him to find his path and also strongly believed the path the he finds, he will show lots of ownership as his own.
- The aim here is to enable the person's overall development in a long term of tenure. Many times the mentor is chosen by the mentee. The pairing is based on (a) The mentee should have trust in that person (if appointed or forced this may not be 100%) (b) The mentee should be inspired by the mentor as role model or provider of that aspired competency (c) The mentee experiences comfort to open and confide each and everything, as the need may be. Often the mentee starts this contracts and the tenure end only at the mentee's instance.

Mentors and coaches are those who passionately believe in the joy of giving and sharing. They stay away from providing prescriptive solutions, instead they are good at questioning skills which are thought provoking. Last but not the least they always show passion and patience for this activity.

Top Tips

- Recall the person who questioned you the most and you cherished undergoing that process.
- Work and build on the questions that you have found useful to discover or identify an unknown side of yours.
- Adopt the qualities of someone who you admired as a role model, for that quality of his/her from which you may have benefited a lot.